Native Docker Clustering Swarm

Deploy, configure, and run clusters of Docker containers
with Swarm

Fabrizio Soppelsa
Chanwit Kaewkasi

BIRMINGHAM - MUMBAI

Native Docker Clustering with Swarm

First published: December 2016

Production reference: 1151216

Published by Packt Publishing Ltd.
Livery Place
35 Livery Street
Birmingham
B3 2PB, UK.
ISBN 978-1-78646-975-5

www.packtpub.com

Credits

Authors
Fabrizio Soppelsa
Chanwit Kaewkasi

Reviewer
Baohua Yang

Commissioning Editor
Wilson D'suoza

Acquisition Editor
Prachi Bisht

Content Development Editor
Trusha Shriyan

Technical Editor
Nirant Carvalho

Copy Editors
Sneha Singh
Laxmi Subramanian

Project Coordinator
Kinjal Bari

Proofreader
Safis Editing

Indexer
Pratik Shirodkar

Graphics
Kirk D'Penha

Production Coordinator
Shantanu N. Zagade

About the Authors

Fabrizio Soppelsa works as an Escalations Engineer for Mirantis Inc., the OpenStack company. Docker activist and advocate since Docker 0.3 and author of several articles on the Docker tools in three languages, he is also a concrete contributor to the projects, especially Machine. He currently lives in Moscow, Russia, where he is the Docker Meetup organizer with his spider Mosha.

I would like to thank ClusterHQ folks for their help on Flocker, especially, Ryan Wallner. the Yandex team and Denis Kutin for having given me a free OpenStack lab on which I could easily access. Mirantis for creating the (I think) best OpenStack distribution. The Docker team and the Docker community, for all the fun.

Chanwit Kaewkasi is an Assistant Professor at the School of Computer Engineering, Suranaree University of Technology, Thailand. Chanwit started contributing to the Docker Swarm project since 0.1 where he co-designed and implemented the strategy filters, the ZooKeeper discovery, and other features. He currently serves as Docker Swarm Maintainer and Docker Captain.

I'd like to thank my wife, Pitchaya, for her encouragement and best support to everything I'm working on, including this book.

Special thanks to the Docker Engineering team for their great software, Suranaree University of Technlogy for being my great workplace, and my parents for their support and lastly, Fabrizio for inviting me to co-author this great book.

About the Reviewer

Baohua Yang is a senior researcher at IBM. His interests include key areas in Cloud Computing, Fintech, distributed system and analytics, especially on emerging technologies, e.g., SDN/NFV, Container, BigData, Blockchain and cognitive computing.

As the chief architect, he has lead the architecture design and system implementation of enterprise productions, and helps solve key technical challenges for industrial solutions.

As an Open-Source contributor, he has submitted code, proposals, and presentations to numbers of projects, e.g., OpenStack, Hyperledger, OpenvSwitch, Docker, OpenDaylight, Kubernetes, and has lead several projects including easyOVS, Hyperledger Fabric-SDK-py and Cello. He is now the chairperson of Hyperledger Technical Working Group in China.

He has published 10s of papers in top-quality international conference and journals (e.g., IEEE INFOCOM, IEEE Trans on Computers), with several technical books and patents. He is now TPC member of numbers of academic conferences and journals.

His homepage is at `https://yeasy.github.com`.

www.PacktPub.com

For support files and downloads related to your book, please visit www.PacktPub.com.

Did you know that Packt offers eBook versions of every book published, with PDF and ePub files available? You can upgrade to the eBook version at www.PacktPub.com and as a print book customer, you are entitled to a discount on the eBook copy. Get in touch with us at service@packtpub.com for more details.

At www.PacktPub.com, you can also read a collection of free technical articles, sign up for a range of free newsletters and receive exclusive discounts and offers on Packt books and eBooks.

https://www.packtpub.com/mapt

Get the most in-demand software skills with Mapt. Mapt gives you full access to all Packt books and video courses, as well as industry-leading tools to help you plan your personal development and advance your career.

Why subscribe?

- Fully searchable across every book published by Packt
- Copy and paste, print, and bookmark content
- On demand and accessible via a web browser

I want to dedicate this book to the memory of my father, Donato.

Table of Contents

Preface

Welcome to Native Docker clustering with Swarm! This is a book about containers and distributed systems. We'll show how to use the native Docker tools to model micro services, spawn tasks, scale up the size of your application, and push your containers to the Docker clustering limit! In a word, we'll discuss Docker orchestration.

With the recent rise of Swarm Mode and the enablement of Swarm inside the Docker Engine itself, it turned out that the best way to orchestrate Docker is… Docker!

Good, but what do we mean by "orchestrate Docker"? What is orchestration? Better, what is an orchestra?

An orchestra is an ensemble of musicians led by a conductor, who dictates tempo, rhythm and shapes the sound. Strings, woodwinds, percussions, keyboards and other instruments follow the conductor's direction to perform an astonishing symphony, for example Beethoven's The Ninth.

Similarly, in a containers orchestration system the musicians are tasks, and the conductor is a leader service (Swarm primitives). Tasks don't play a symphony, or at least not only: More abstractly they execute some computational job, for example they run a webserver. The conductor, Swarm, is responsible for their provisioning, their availability, their linkage, their scaling. This (and more) is what we mean by "Docker orchestration".

This book shows how to provision such Docker "orchestras", how to guarantee the availability of the service, how to connect tasks and how to scale the platform, to play the symphony of your application.

What this book covers

Chapter 1, *Welcome to Docker Swarm*, introduces Swarm, and explains why you need a clustering solution for your containers. It illustrates the Swarm features, giving a high-level description of its architecture. We define some use cases and describe how Swarm is different from Fleet, Kubernetes and Mesos. The chapter proceeds with the Docker tools installation and finally with two Swarms provisionings: A local Swarm Standalone and a remote Swarm Mode cluster on DigitalOcean.

Chapter 2, *Discover the Discovery Services*, is a descriptive and mostly abstract chapter. We'll learn what discovery mechanisms and consensus algorithms are, and why they are crucial for distributed systems. We'll describe in detail Raft and its implementation Etcd, the consensus mechanism included in Swarm Mode. We will also show the limitations of the discovery mechanism used in Chapter 1, *Welcome to Docker Swarm*, by extending the local tiny example with Consul, re deploying it.

Chapter 3, *Meeting Docker Swarm Mode*, is about the new Docker kit that allows to create task clusters of any size. We will introduce Swarmit, the foundation of Docker Swarm Mode, showing how it works in Docker 1.12+, discuss its architecture, its concepts, how it's different from the "old" Swarm, and how it organizes workloads by abstracting services and tasks.

Chapter 4, *Creating a Production-Grade Swarm*, shows and discusses the community-driven projects Swarm2k and Swarm3k, our 2,300 and 4,800 nodes Swarm clusters experiments, which ran hundreds of thousands of containers. We demonstrate how such huge clusters were planned, provisioned, and summarize the lessons we learned.

`Chapter` 5, *Administer a Swarm Cluster*, is a chapter about infrastructure. We will show how to increase or decrease Swarms sizes, how to promote and demote nodes, and how to update clusters and nodes properties. We'll introduce Shipyard and Portainer.io as graphical UIs for Swarm.

`Chapter` 6, *Deploy Real Applications on Swarm*, is where we will put real applications in motion on Swarm and where we add to the discussion some notes about Compose, Docker Stacks and Docker Application Bundles. We will show the typical deployment workflow, how to filter and schedule containers over the cluster, launch them as services, handle containers as tasks. We'll start defining a web service with Nginx, then we'll deploy a mandatory Wordpress with MySQL example. We'll finally move on with a more realistic app: Apache Spark.

`Chapter` 7, *Scale Up Your Platform*, will develop new topics from the previous chapter. Here we'll introduce Flocker to add storage capacity to Spark on Swarm, and we'll show how to install and use it automatically at a scale in conjunction with Swarm. We'll refine our Spark example by running some real big data jobs and setting up a basic monitoring system for this infrastructure.

`Chapter` 8, *Exploring Additional Features to Swarm*, discusses some advanced topics important to Swarm, such as Libnetwork and Libkv.

`Chapter` 9, *Securing a Swarm Cluster and Docker Software Supply Chain*, will focus on security considerations for Swarm clusters. Among the arguments, certificates, firewalling concepts for platform, and a mention to Notary.

`Chapter` 10, *Swarm and the Cloud*, is a chapter illustrating the most popular options for running Swarm on cloud providers. We'll install Swarm on AWS and Azure before introducing the Docker Datacenter, and we'll finally move to OpenStack showing how to install and manage Swarms on the top of Magnum, the Container as a Service solution for OpenStack.

`Chapter` 11, *What is Next?*, concludes the discussion with an overview on the next Docker orchestration trends, such as software defined infrastructures, Infrakit, unikernels, Containers as a Service. The adventure continues!

What you need for this book

We assume the reader to have some experience using Docker from the command line: throughout the book we'll continuously pull images, run containers, define services, expose ports and create networks.

Also, the ideal reader possesses a basic understanding of networking protocols and is familiar with public and private cloud concepts like virtual machines and tenant networks.

To follow the examples in the text, you will need Docker and its tools. Chapter 1, *Welcome to Docker Swarm*, covers their installation.

Also, to get the most from the examples, you will need access to a a public (for example AWS, Azure or DigitalOcean) or private (for example OpenStack) cloud to instantiate Virtual Machines.

Who this book is for

This book is for Docker users - developers and system administrators - who want to exploit the current Swarm and Swarmkit features for scaling massive applications with containers.

Conventions

In this book, you will find a number of text styles that distinguish between different kinds of information. Here are some examples of these styles and an explanation of their meaning.

Code words in text, database table names, folder names, filenames, file extensions, pathnames, dummy URLs, user input, and Twitter handles are shown as follows: "When executing docker swarm init, just copy-paste the lines printed as output"

A block of code is set as follows:

```
digitalocean:
    image: "docker-1.12-rc4"
    region: nyc3
    ssh_key_fingerprint: "your SSH ID"
    ssh_user: root
```

Any command-line input or output is written as follows:

```
# Set $GOPATH here
go get https://github.com/chanwit/belt
```

New terms and **important words** are shown in bold. Words that you see on the screen, for example, in menus or dialog boxes, appear in the text like this: "The UI has the expected options, included a list of templates for launching containers, such as **MySQL** or a **Private Registry**, but at the moment of writing it doesn't support Swarm services yet"

Warnings or important notes appear in a box like this.

Tips and tricks appear like this.

Reader feedback

Feedback from our readers is always welcome. Let us know what you think about this book-what you liked or disliked. Reader feedback is important for us as it helps us develop titles that you will really get the most out of. To send us general feedback, simply e-mail feedback@packtpub.com, and mention the book's title in the subject of your message. If there is a topic that you have expertise in and you are interested in either writing or contributing to a book, see our author guide at www.packtpub.com/authors.

Customer support

Now that you are the proud owner of a Packt book, we have a number of things to help you to get the most from your purchase.

Errata

Although we have taken every care to ensure the accuracy of our content, mistakes do happen. If you find a mistake in one of our books-maybe a mistake in the text or the code-we would be grateful if you could report this to us. By doing so, you can save other readers from frustration and help us improve subsequent versions of this book. If you find any errata, please report them by visiting http://www.packtpub.com/submit-errata, selecting your book, clicking on the **Errata Submission Form** link, and entering the details of your errata. Once your errata are verified, your submission will be accepted and the errata will be uploaded to our website or added to any list of existing errata under the Errata section of that title.

To view the previously submitted errata, go to `https://www.packtpub.com/books/conten t/support`and enter the name of the book in the search field. The required information will appear under the **Errata** section.

Piracy

Piracy of copyrighted material on the Internet is an ongoing problem across all media. At Packt, we take the protection of our copyright and licenses very seriously. If you come across any illegal copies of our works in any form on the Internet, please provide us with the location address or website name immediately so that we can pursue a remedy.

Please contact us at `copyright@packtpub.com` with a link to the suspected pirated material.

We appreciate your help in protecting our authors and our ability to bring you valuable content.

"Illustrations of Swarm Architecture, Minimal Swarm on Production, and Docker Eco System in `Chapter 1`, *Welcome to Docker Swarm* © 2015-2016 Docker, Inc. Used by permission."

Questions

If you have a problem with any aspect of this book, you can contact us at `questions@packtpub.com`, and we will do our best to address the problem.

1
Welcome to Docker Swarm

It's no mystery that Docker is one of the open-source technologies that have the most traction nowadays. The reasons are easy to understand, Docker makes the container technology available for all, and it comes with an included battery that is removable and is blessed by a vibrant community.

In the early days, users started working with Docker after being fascinated with this easy-to-use tool, which allowed them to sort out many challenges: pulling, packing, isolating, and making applications portable across systems with almost no burden.

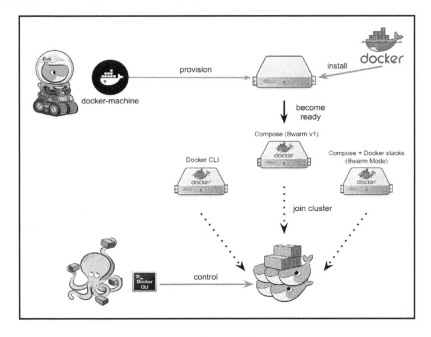

A simplified Docker Ecosystem

You may notice a swarm of whales here plays nice with others. However, since the advent of containers, people have been looking for tools to efficiently orchestrate a huge number of them. The Docker team addressed this necessity with the release of Docker Swarm, hereinafter Swarm, one of the pieces of the Docker ecosystem, in 2015, alongside with Docker Machine and Docker Compose. The preceding image shows the simplified Docker Ecosystem, which consists of Docker Machine provisioning a new Docker-ready machine, then a set of machines will be formed into a Docker Swarm cluster. Later we will be able to use Docker Compose to deploy containers to the cluster, as if it were a normal Docker Engine.

The plan to make a cluster management system, natively, for Docker started in early 2014, as a communication protocol project called *Beam*. Later, it was implemented as a daemon to control heterogeneous distributed systems with the Docker API. The project had been renamed to `libswarm` and `Swarmd` is its daemon. Keeping the same concept of allowing any Docker client to connect to a pool of Docker Engines, the third generation of the project had been re-designed to use the same set of Docker Remote APIs and renamed to "Swarm" in November 2014. Basically, the most important part of Swarm are its remote APIs; the maintainers work hard to keep them 100% compatible with every version of Docker Engine. We'll call the first generation of Swarm as "Swarm v1".

In February 2016, after the core team found the scaling limitation of the centralized service, Swarm has been internally redesigned again as `swarm.v2`. This time, a decentralized cluster design has been taken into account. In June 2016, SwarmKit had been released as the orchestration toolkit for distributed service at any scale. Docker announced that SwarmKit was merged into Docker Engine at DockerCon 2016. We'll refer to this version of Swarm as "Swarm v2" or "Swarm mode".

As we'll see later, these three musketeers (Docker Swarm, Docker Machine, and Docker Compose) operate best when together and they are so seamlessly intertwined with each other that it is almost impossible to think of them as single pieces.

However, even despite this Machine and Compose are really direct in their goals and easy to use and understand, Swarm is a tool that indeed deserves a book for itself.

With Docker Machine, you can provision machines, both virtual and physical, on a number of cloud platforms as well as bare metal machines to run Docker containers. With Docker Compose, you can define Dockerfiles on steroids, by describing behaviors with the easy yet powerful syntax of YAML and launch applications by just "composing up" these files. Swarm is a powerful clustering tool that requires to be studied more in depth.

In this chapter, we will be taking a look at the following topics:

- What is container orchestration
- Docker Swarm fundamentals and architecture
- Differences with other open source orchestrators
- The "old" Swarm, v1
- The "new" Swarm, Swarm Mode

Clustering tools and container managers

A clustering tool is software that allows an operator to talk to a single end point and to command and *orchestrate* a set of resources, in our case containers. Instead of manually distributing workloads (containers) on a cluster, a clustering tool is used to automate this and many other tasks. It's the clustering tool that will decide *where* to start jobs (containers), *how* to store them, *when* to eventually restart them, and so on. The operator needs to only configure some behaviors, decide the cluster topology and size, tune settings, and enable or disable advanced features. Docker Swarm is an example of clustering tool for containers.

Beyond clustering tools, there is also a choice of container manager platforms. They do not provide container hosting, but interact with one or more existing systems; this kind of software usually offer good web interfaces, monitoring tools, and other visual or higher-level functionalities. Examples of container manager platforms are Rancher or Tutum (acquired in 2015 by Docker Inc.).

Swarm goals

Swarm is described by Docker itself as:

> *Docker Swarm is native clustering for Docker. It turns a pool of Docker hosts into a single, virtual Docker host.*

Swarm is a tool that gives you the illusion to manage a single-huge Docker host made of many Docker hosts, as they were one and had one command-entry point. It allows you to orchestrate and operate a certain number of containers on these hosts, using the routine Docker tools, either using the Docker native or the python-docker client, even curl with the Docker Remote APIs.

This is what a minimal Swarm cluster in production looks similar to:

Why use Swarm

There are many reasons to use a clustering solution for your containers. As you will see your applications growing, you will face new mandatory requirements, such as scalability, manageability, and high availability.

There are many tools available out there; picking up Docker Swarm gives us some immediate advantages:

- **Native clustering**: Swarm is a native in Docker and made by the Docker team and community. Its original creators are Andrea Luzzardi and Victor Vieux, who are the early implementers of Docker Engine Remote API itself. Swarm integrates, with no additional requirements, with Machine, Compose, and the other tools from the ecosystem.

- **Production grade**: Swarm v1 was declared mature in November 2015 and is ready to be used in production. The team already demonstrated that Swarm can scale-up to control Engines that are as large as 1,000 nodes. Swarm v2 allows forming clusters with multi-thousand nodes, as it uses a decentralized discovery.
- **Work out-of-the-box**: Swarm does not require you to re-architect your app to adapt to another orchestration tool. You can use your Docker images and configurations with no changes and deploy them at a scale.
- **Easy to setup and use**: Swarm is easy to operate. Effective deployments can be done by just adding some flags to Machine commands or using Docker commands since Docker 1.12. Discovery service is integrated into Swarm Mode, making it quick to install: There is no need to set up external Consul, Etcd, or Zookeeper clusters.
- **Active community**: Swarm is a vibrant project, with a very active community and is under heavy development.
- **Available on Hub**: You don't need to install Swarm, it comes ready as a Docker image (Swarm v1), and so you just pull and run it from the Hub or integrated into the Docker Engine. While Swarm Mode is already integrated into Docker 1.12+. That's all.

Real world use case examples

Docker Swarm is the choice of several projects, for example:

- Rackspace Carina is built atop Docker Swarm: Rackspace offers hosted container environment, which is internally based on Docker Swarm
- Zenly is using Swarm across Google Cloud Platform and bare metal servers
- ADP uses Docker and Swarm to give velocity to their legacy deployments
- Swarms can be deployed with Amazon AWS and Microsoft Azure templates directly on their public clouds

Pet versus cattle models

There are two opposite approaches when creating and utilizing infrastructures: pet versus cattle.

In the *pet* model, the administrator deploys servers or virtual machines or, in our case, containers and takes care of them. She or he logs in, installs software, configures it, and ensures that everything is working fine. As a result, this is her or his pet.

By contrast, the administrator doesn't really care about the destiny of his infrastructural components, when thinking of them as *cattles*. She or he doesn't log in to every single unit or handle it manually, rather, uses a bulk approach, deployment, configuration, and management are done with automation tools. If a server or container dies, it's automatically resurrected, or another is generated to substitute for the defunct. As a result, the operator is handling cattle.

In this book, we'll use the pet model in the very first chapter to introduce some basic concepts to the reader. But we'll follow the cattle pattern later, when it will be the time to do serious things.

Swarm features

The main purpose of Swarm was already defined, but how does it accomplish its goals? Here are its key features:

- Swarm v1 supports Docker Engine of version 1.6.0 or more recent. Swarm v2 has been in built for Docker Engine since version 1.12.
- APIs of each release of Swarm will be compatible with Docker APIs on the same release train. API compatibility is maintained for one version backward.
- In Swarm v1, the leader-election mechanism is implemented for multiple Swarm masters using the leadership library (only supported when deploying Swarm with a discovery service, such as Etcd, Consul, or Zookeeper).
- In Swarm v2, leader election has been built using the decentralized mechanism. Swarm v2 does not need a dedicated set of discovery services anymore because it integrates Etcd, an implementation of the Raft consensus algorithm (see `Chapter 2`, *Discover the Discovery Services*).
- In the Swarm v1 terminology, the leader Swarm master is called primary, where others are called replica. In Swarm v2, there is a concept of Master and Worker nodes. While the leader nodes are managed automatically by the cluster using Raft.
- Basic and advanced scheduling options. The scheduler is an algorithm that decides the hosts on which the containers must be physically placed. Swarm comes with a set of built-in schedulers.
- Constraints and affinities to let the operator take decisions on scheduling; for example, one wants to keep the database containers geographically near and suggest the scheduler to do that. Constraints and affinities use Docker Swarm labels.

- In Swarm v2, in-cluster load balancing is implemented with the built-in DNS Round-Robin, while it supports external load balancing via the routing mesh mechanism, which is implemented over IPVS.
- High-availability and failover mechanism means that you can create a Swarm with more than one master; so if they go down, there will be other master/s ready to take control. Swarm v2 is available, by default, when we form a cluster of at least 3 nodes. All nodes can be the master nodes. Also, Swarm v2 includes health indicator information.

Similar projects

We have more than only Docker Swarm out there to clusterize containers. For completeness, we will briefly review the most widely known open source alternatives, before diving completely into Swarm.

Kubernetes

Kubernetes (http://kubernetes.io), also known as **k8s**, aims at the same goal of Docker Swarm; it's a manager for cluster of containers. Started originally as project Borg in Google laboratories, it was later open sourced and released as a stable version in 2015, supporting **Google Cloud Platform**, **CoreOS**, **Azure**, and **vSphere**.

Kubernetes so far runs containers in Docker, which is commanded via API by a so called Kubelet, a service that registers and manages Pods. Architecturally, Kubernetes divides its clusters, logically, not into bare containers but into Pods. A Pod is the smallest deployable unit and is physically a representation of an application made by a group of one or more containers, usually collocated, that share resources such as storage and networking (users can simulate Pods in Docker using Compose and starting from Docker 1.12 create Docker **DABs** (**Distributed Application Bundles**)).

Kubernetes includes some expected basic clustering features, such as labels, health checkers, Pods registry, has configurable schedulers, and services such as ambassadors or load balancers.

In practice, the Kubernetes user utilizes the kubectl client to interface to the Kubernetes master, the cluster controlling unit that commands the Kubernetes nodes doing some work, called minions. Minions run Pods and everything is glued by Etcd.

On a Kubernetes node, you will find a running Docker Engine, which runs a kube-api container, and a system service called `kubelet.service`.

There are a of kubectl commands that are pretty intuitive, such as

- `kubectl cluster-info`, `kubectl get pods`, and `kubectl get nodes` to retrieve information about the cluster and its health
- `kubectl create -f cassandra.yaml` and any derivative Pod commands, to create, manage, and destroy Pods
- `kubectl scale rc cassandra --replicas=2` to scale Pods and applications
- `kubectl label pods cassandra env=prod` to configure Pod labels

This is just a high level panoramic of Kubernetes. The main differences between Kubernetes and Docker Swarm are:

- Swarm has a more straightforward architecture to understand. Kubernetes requires more focus, just to grasp its fundamentals. But studying is always good!
- Again on architecture: Kubernetes is based on Pods, Swarm on containers, and DABs.
- You need to install Kubernetes. By either deploying on GCE, using CoreOS, or on the top of OpenStack, you must take care of it. You must deploy and configure a Kubernetes cluster, and this is some little extra effort. Swarm is integrated into Docker, and requires no extra installations.
- Kubernetes has an additional concept of Replication Controllers, a technology that ensure that all the Pods described by some templates are running at a given time.
- Both Kubernetes and Swarm use Etcd. But while in Kubernetes it's treated as an external facility service, in Swarm it's integrated and runs on manager nodes.

A performance comparison between Kubernetes and Swarm might take form of holy wars and we want to subtract to this practice. There are benchmarks showing how fast is Swarm in starting containers and other benchmarks showing how fast is Kubernetes in running its workloads. We are of the opinion that benchmark results must always be taken *cum grano salis*. That said, both Kubernetes and Swarm are suitable for running big, fast, and scalable containers clusters.

CoreOS Fleet

Fleet (`https://github.com/coreos/fleet`) is another possible choice amongst container orchestrators. It comes from the family of CoreOS container products (which includes CoreOS, Rocket, and Flannel) and is basically different from Swarm, Kubernetes, and Mesos in that it's architected as an extension to system. Fleet operates through schedulers to distribute resources and tasks across the cluster nodes. Hence, its goal is not only to provide a pure containers clusterization rather to be a distributed more general elaboration system. It's possible, for example, to run Kubernetes on the top of Fleet.

A Fleet cluster is made of engines responsible for scheduling jobs, other management operations, and agents, running on each host, that are physically executing the jobs they're assigned and reporting the status continuously to engines. Etcd is the discovery services that keeps everything glued.

You interact through a Fleet cluster with its main command `fleetctl`, with the list, start, and stop containers and services options.

So, summarising, Fleet is different from Docker Swarm:

- It's a higher-level abstraction that distributes tasks, it's not a mere container orchestrator.
- Think of Fleet as more of a distributed init system for your cluster. Systemd is for one host, Fleet for a cluster of hosts.
- Fleet clusterizes specifically a bunch of CoreOS nodes
- You can run Kubernetes on the top of Fleet to exploit Fleet features of resiliency and high availability
- There are no known stable and robust ways to integrate Fleet and Swarm v1 automatically.
- Currently, Fleet is not tested to run clusters with more than 100 nodes and 1000 containers (`https://github.com/coreos/fleet/blob/master/Documentation/fleet-scaling.md`) while we were able to run Swarms with 2300 and later 4500 nodes.

Apache Mesos

Whether you can see Fleet as a distributed init system for your cluster, you can think of Mesos (`https://mesos.apache.org/`) in terms of a *distributed kernel*. With Mesos, you can make available all your nodes resources as if they were one and, for the scope of this book, run containers clusters on them.

Mesos, originally started at the University of Berkeley in 2009, is a mature project and has been used in production with success, for example by Twitter.

It's even more general purpose than Fleet, being multi-platform (you can run it on Linux, OS X or Windows nodes) and capable of running heterogeneous jobs. You can typically have clusters of containers running on Mesos just aside of pure Big Data jobs (Hadoop or Spark) and others, including continuous integration, real-time processing, web applications, data storage, and even more.

A Mesos cluster is made of one Master, slaves, and frameworks. As you would expect, the master allocates resources and tasks on the slaves, it is responsible for the system communications and runs a discovery service (ZooKeeper). But what are frameworks? Frameworks are applications. A framework is made of a scheduler and an executor, the first one distributes tasks and the second executes them.

For our interest, typically containers are run on Mesos through a framework named Marathon (`https://mesosphere.github.io/marathon/docs/native-docker.html`).

A comparison between Mesos and Docker Swarm does not make sense here, since they may very well run complementarily, that is Docker Swarm v1 can run on Mesos and a portion of Swarm source code is just dedicated to this. Swarm Mode and SwarmKit, instead, are very similar to Mesos since they abstract jobs in tasks and group them in services, to distribute loads on the cluster. We'll discuss better of SwarmKit features in `Chapter 3`, *Meeting Docker Swarm Mode*.

Kubernetes versus Fleet versus Mesos

Kubernetes, Fleet and Mesos try to address a similar problem; they provide a layer abstraction for your resources and allow you to interface to a cluster manager. Then you can launch jobs and tasks and the project of your choice will sort it out. The difference can be seen in the features provided out-of-the-box and on how much you can customize the precision of allocating and scaling resources and jobs. Of the three, Kubernetes is more automatic, Mesos more customizable so, from a certain point of view, powerful (if you need all that power, of course).

Kubernetes and Fleet abstract and make default many details that for Mesos are needed to be configured, for example a scheduler. On Mesos, you can use the Marathon or Chronos scheduler or even write your own. If you don't require, don't want or even can't dig deep into those technicalities, you can pick up Kubernetes or Fleet. It depends on your actual and/or forecasted workload.

Swarm versus all

So, what solution should you adopt? As always, you have a problem and open source is generous enough to make many technologies available that can often intersect on to each other, to help you successfully reach a goal. The problem is how and what to choose to resolve your problem. Kubernetes, Fleet, and Mesos are all powerful and interesting projects and so is Docker Swarm.

In a hypothetic standing of how automatic and simple to understand these four guys are, Swarm is a winner. This is not an advantage always, but in this book we'll show how Docker Swarm can help you to make real things work, bearing in mind that in one of the DockerCon keynotes Solomon Hykes, CTO and Founder of Docker, suggested that *Swarm would be a tier that could provide a common interface onto the many orchestration and scheduling frameworks.*

The Swarm v1 architecture

This section discusses the overview architecture of Docker Swarm. The internal structure of Swarm is described in Figure 3.

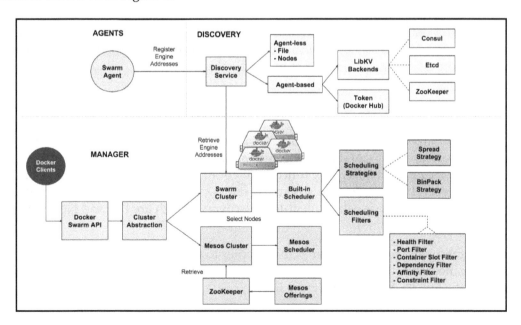

The internal structure of Docker Swarm v1

Starting with the **MANAGER** part, you will see a block labeled with *Docker Swarm API* on the left-side of the diagram. As mentioned previously, Swarm exposes the set of remote APIs similar to Docker, which allows you to use any Docker clients to connect to Swarm. However, the Swarm APIs are slightly different from the standard Docker Remote APIs, as Swarm APIs contains cluster-related information too. For example, running `docker info` against Docker Engine will give you the information of the single Engine, but when we call `docker info` against a Swarm cluster, we'll also get the number of nodes in the cluster as well as each node's information and health.

The block next to Docker Swarm API is *Cluster Abstraction*. It is an abstraction layer to allow different kinds of cluster to be implemented as backend of Swarm and share the same set of Docker Remote APIs. Currently we have two cluster backend, the built-in Swarm cluster implementation and the Mesos cluster implementation. *Swarm Cluster* and *Built-in Scheduler* blocks represent the built-in Swarm cluster implementation, while the blocks denoted by *Mesos Cluster* is the Mesos cluster implementation.

The *Built-in Scheduler* of the Swarm backend comes with a number of *Scheduling Strategies*. Two strategies are *Spread* and *BinPack*, which will be explained in the later chapters. If you're familiar with Swarm, you will note that the Random strategy is missing here. The Random strategy is excluded from the explanation as it is for testing purpose only.

Along with Scheduling Strategies, Swarm employs a set of *Scheduling Filters* to help screening criteria-unmet nodes out. There are currently six kinds of filter namely, *Health*, *Port*, *Container Slots*, *Dependency*, *Affinity*, and *Constraint*. They are applied to filter when one is scheduling the newly created container in exactly this order.

On the **AGENTS** part, there are Swarm agents trying to register address of their Engines into the discovery service.

Finally, the centralized piece, **DISCOVERY**, is to coordinate addresses of the Engines between AGENTS and MANAGER. The agent-based Discovery Service currently uses LibKV, which delegates the discovery function to your key-value store of choices, Consul, Etcd, or ZooKeeper. In contrast, we also can use only Docker Swarm manager without any key-value store. This mode is called agent-less discovery, which are File and Nodes (specify address on the command line).

We will use the agent-less model later in this chapter to create a minimal local Swarm cluster. We'll meet the other discovery services starting in `Chapter 2`, *Discover the Discovery Services* and the Swarm Mode architecture in `Chapter 3`, *Meeting Docker Swarm Mode*.

Terminology

Before continuing to other sections, we review some Docker-related terminologies to recall Docker concepts and introduce Swarm keywords.

- A **Docker Engine** is a Docker daemon running on a host machine. Sometimes in the book we'll just refer to it as Engine. We usually start an Engine by calling `docker daemon` via systemd or other start up services.

- **Docker Compose** is a tool to describe in YAML how multi-container services must be architected.

- **Docker stacks** are the binary result of creating images of multiple-containers app (described by Compose) instead of single containers.

- A **Docker daemon** is an interchangeable term with Docker Engine.

- A **Docker client** is the client program packed in the same docker executable. For example, when we do `docker run`, we are using the Docker client.

- **Docker networking** is a Software-defined Network that links a set of containers in the same network together. By default, we'll use the libnetwork (`https://github.com/docker/libnetwork`) implementation came with Docker Engine. But you can optionally deploy third-party network drivers of your choices using plugins.

- **Docker Machine** is a tool used to create hosts capable of running Docker Engines called **machines**.

- A **Swarm node in Swarm v1** is a machine that is a pre-installed Docker Engine and has a Swarm agent program running alongside. A Swarm node will register itself into a Discovery service.

- A **Swarm master in Swarm v1** is a machine that is running a Swarm manager program. A Swarm master reads addresses of Swarm nodes from its Discovery service.

- A **Discovery service** is a token-based service offered by Docker or a self-hosted one. For the self-hosted ones, you can run HashiCorp Consul, CoreOS Etcd, or Apache ZooKeeper as key-value stores to serve as the discovery service.

- **Leader Election** is a mechanism done by Swarm Masters to find the primary node. Other master nodes will be in the replica role until the primary node goes down and then the leader election process will start again. As we'll see, the number of Swarm masters should be an odd number.

- **SwarmKit** is a new Kit released by Docker to abstract orchestration. Theoretically, it should be able run *any* kind of service but in practice so far it orchestrates only containers and sets of containers.
- **Swarm Mode** is the new Swarm, available since Docker 1.12, that integrates SwarmKit into the Docker Engine.
- **Swarm Master (in Swarm Mode)** is a node that manages the cluster: It schedules services, keeps the cluster configuration (nodes, roles, and labels) and ensures that there is a cluster leader.
- **Swarm Worker (in Swarm Mode)** is a node which runs tasks, for example, hosts containers.
- **Services** are abstractions of workloads. For example, we can have a service "nginx" replicated 10 times, meaning that you will have 10 tasks (10 nginx containers) distributed on the cluster and load balanced by Swarm itself
- **Tasks** are the unit of work of Swarms. A task is a container.

Getting started with Swarm

We'll now proceed with the installation of two small Swarm v1 and v2 proof of concept clusters, the first on local and the second on Digital Ocean. In order to execute the recipes, check the list of ingredients, ensure that you have everything, and then begin.

To follow the example, you'll need:

- Either a Windows, Mac OS X, or Linux desktop
- A Bash or Bash-compatible shell. On Windows you can either useCygwin or Git Bash.
- The latest version of VirtualBox, installed for the local example
- At least 4GB of memory for 4 VirtualBox instances of 1G of memory each for the local example
- A Docker client, at least version 1.6.0 for Swarm v1 and 1.12 for Swarm v2
- The latest version of Docker Machine, which is currently 0.8.1

Docker for Mac

Docker announced the desktop version of Docker for Mac and Docker for Windows early in 2016. It's better than the Docker Toolbox, since it includes the Docker CLI tools you expect but doesn't use boot2docker and VirtualBox anymore (it uses unikernels instead, which we'll introduce in `Chapter 11`, *What is Next?*) and it's fully integrated into the operating system (Mac OS X Sierra or Windows 10 with Hyper-V enabled).

You can download the Docker desktop from `https://www.docker.com/products/overview#/install_the_platform`and install it easily.

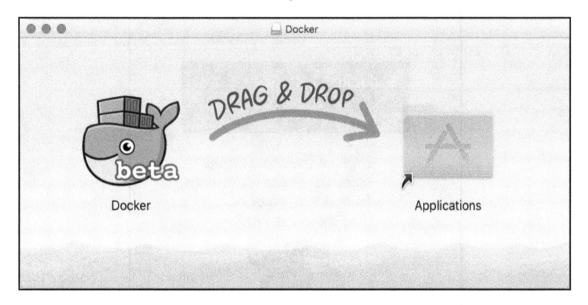

Just drag and drop the Docker beta icon to your applications folder if you're using Mac OS X. Input your beta registration code, if any, and it's done.

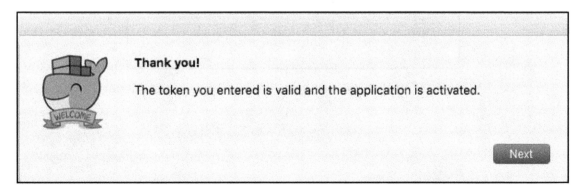

On OS X, you will have the Docker whale in the system tray, which you can open and also configure your settings. A Docker host will be running natively on your desktop.

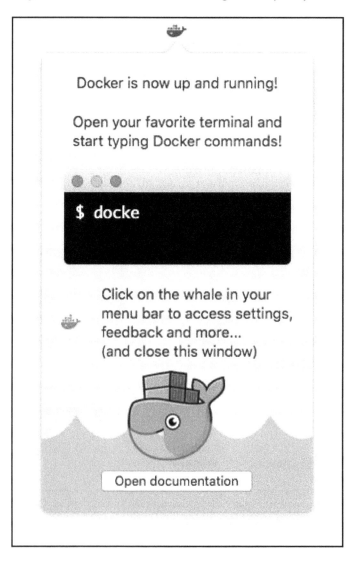

Docker for Windows

In the case of Docker for Windows, it requires Windows 10 with Hyper-V enabled. Basically, Hyper-V comes with Windows 10 Professional or higher versions. After double-clicking on the setup program, you'll see that the first screen, showing the License Agreement, looks similar to the following screenshot. The setup program will request you for a key similar to that of Docker for Mac.

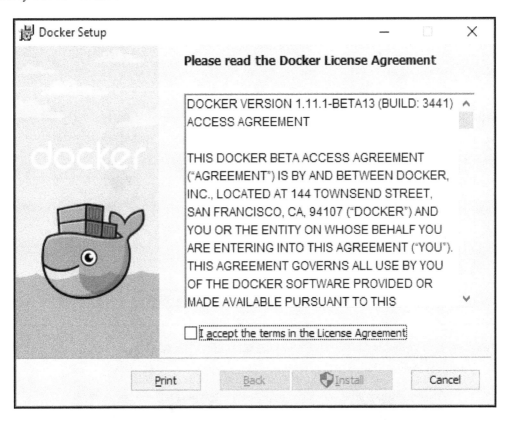

If the installation process goes smoothly, you will see that the finish screen is ready for you to launch Docker for Windows, as shown:

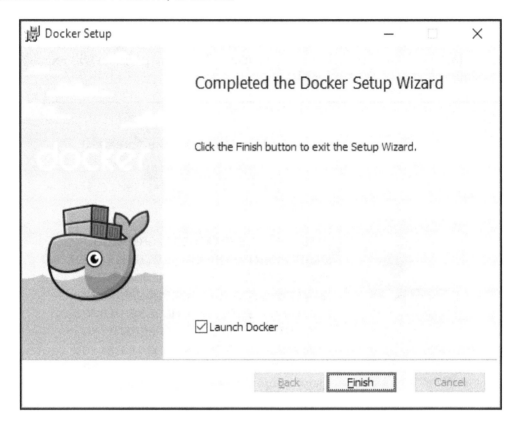

At the time of launch, Docker will initialize itself to the Hyper-V. Once the process is done, you can just open PowerShell and start using Docker.

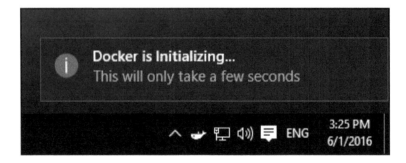

If something goes wrong you can open the logging Windows from the tray icon's menu, as well as check with Hyper-V Manager.

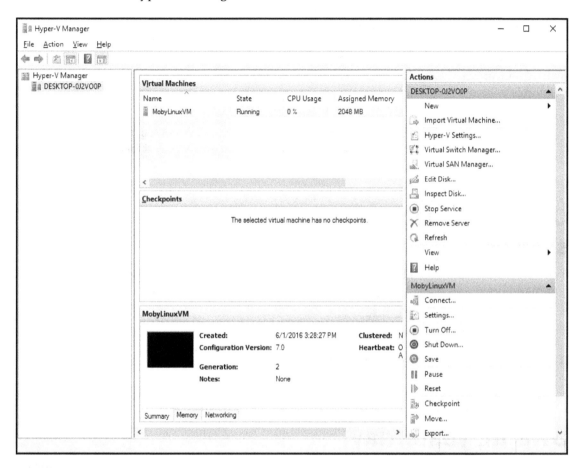

Getting ready with Linux

We'll extensively use Machine in this book, so ensure that you have it installed through Docker for Mac or Windows or Docker Toolbox. If you use Linux on your desktop, install the Docker client with your package system (apt or rpm). You will also have to download the bare machine binary, just curl it and assign it the execution permissions; follow the instructions at `https://docs.docker.com/machine/install-machine/`. The current stable version is 0.8.1.

```
$ curl -L
https://github.com/docker/machine/releases/download/v0.8.1/docker-
machine-uname -s-uname -m > /usr/local/bin/docker-machine
$ chmod +x /usr/local/bin/docker-machine`
```

Check that Docker Machine is available – all systems

You can check that the machine is ready to be used with the following command from the command line:

```
$ docker-machine --version
docker-machine version 0.8.1, build 41b3b25
```

If you have problems, please control the system paths or download the correct binary for your architecture.

Swarm, yesterday

For the very first example, we'll run the easiest possible configuration of a Swarm v1 cluster locally to get a taste of how "old" Swarms worked (and still works). This tiny cluster will have the following features:

- Made of four nodes of 1CPU, 1GB of memory each, it will consist of an infrastructure of four CPUs and 4GB of memory available in total
- Each node will run on VirtualBox
- Each node is connected to each other on the local VirtualBox network
- No discovery service is involved: a static `nodes://` mechanism will be used
- No security is configured, in other words TLS is disabled

Our cluster will look similar to the following diagram. Four Engines will be connected to each other through port 3376 in a mesh. Beyond the Docker engine, in fact, each of them will run a Docker container exposing port 3376 (Swarm) on host and redirecting it into itself. We, operators, will be able to connect to (any of) the hosts by setting the environment variable DOCKER_HOST to IP:3376. Everything will become clearer if you follow the example step-by-step.

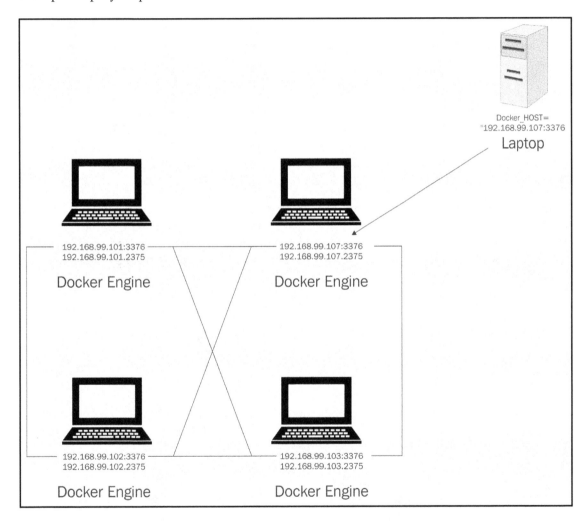

To begin, we must create four Docker hosts with Docker Machine. Docker Machine automates these steps with one command instead of manually creating a Linux VM, generating and uploading certificates, logging into it via SSH, and installing and configuring the Docker daemon.

Machine will perform the following steps:

1. Spin up a VirtualBox VM starting from the boot2docker image.
2. Assign the VM an IP on the VirtualBox internal network.
3. Upload and configure certificates and keys.
4. Install Docker daemon on this VM.
5. Configure the Docker daemon and expose it so it will be remotely reachable.

As a result, we'll have a VM running Docker and ready to be accessed to run containers.

Boot2Docker

Built with Tiny Core Linux, **Boot2Docker** is a lightweight distribution, which is especially designed for running Docker containers. It's runs completely on RAM and the boot time is extremely fast, around five seconds from start to the console. When starting the Engine, Boot2Docker starts Docker Engine at the secure port 2376 by default.

Boot2Docker is by no mean for the production workload. It's designed for development and testing purpose only. We'll start with using boot2docker then later move on to the production in subsequent chapters. At the time of writing, Boot2Docker supports Docker 1.12.3 and uses Linux Kernel 4.4. It comes with AUFS 4 as the default storage driver for Docker Engine.

Create 4 cluster nodes with Docker Machine

If we execute:

```
$ docker-machine ls
```

on our new installation to list the available machines, we see that we have no running ones.

So, let's start by creating one, with this command:

```
$ docker-machine create --driver virtualbox node0
```

This command specifically asks to use the VirtualBox driver (-d for short) and to name the machine node0. Docker Machines can provision machines on dozens of different public and private providers, such as AWS, DigitalOcean, Azure, OpenStack, and has lots of options. For now, we go with the standard settings. The first cluster node will be ready after some time.

At this point, issue the following command to get a control of this host (so to remotely gain access):

```
$ docker-machine env node0
```

This will print some shell variables. Just copy the last row, the one with eval, paste it and issue enter. With those variables configured, you are not operating the local daemon anymore (if any), but the Docker daemon of `node0`.

```
darthvader:~ fsoppelsa$ docker-machine ls
NAME    ACTIVE   DRIVER   STATE   URL   SWARM   DOCKER   ERRORS
darthvader:~ fsoppelsa$ docker-machine create --driver virtualbox node0
Running pre-create checks...
Creating machine...
(node0) Copying /Users/fsoppelsa/.docker/machine/cache/boot2docker.iso to /Users/fsoppelsa/.docker/machine/machines/node0/boot2
docker.iso...
(node0) Creating VirtualBox VM...
(node0) Creating SSH key...
(node0) Starting the VM...
(node0) Check network to re-create if needed...
(node0) Waiting for an IP...
Waiting for machine to be running, this may take a few minutes...
Detecting operating system of created instance...
Waiting for SSH to be available...
Detecting the provisioner...
Provisioning with boot2docker...
Copying certs to the local machine directory...
Copying certs to the remote machine...
Setting Docker configuration on the remote daemon...
Checking connection to Docker...
Docker is up and running!
To see how to connect your Docker Client to the Docker Engine running on this virtual machine, run: docker-machine env node0
darthvader:~ fsoppelsa$ docker-machine env node0
export DOCKER_TLS_VERIFY="1"
export DOCKER_HOST="tcp://192.168.99.107:2376"
export DOCKER_CERT_PATH="/Users/fsoppelsa/.docker/machine/machines/node0"
export DOCKER_MACHINE_NAME="node0"
# Run this command to configure your shell:
# eval $(docker-machine env node0)
darthvader:~ fsoppelsa$ eval $(docker-machine env node0)
darthvader:~ fsoppelsa$ ▮
```

If you check the list of machines again, you will see a * next to the image name, to indicate that it's the machine currently in use. Alternatively, you can type the following command to print the currently active machine:

```
$ docker-machine active
```

```
darthvader:~ fsoppelsa$ docker-machine active
node0
darthvader:~ fsoppelsa$ docker-machine ls
NAME    ACTIVE   DRIVER       STATE     URL                            SWARM   DOCKER    ERRORS
node0   *        virtualbox   Running   tcp://192.168.99.107:2376              v1.11.1
```

The daemon is running on this machine, with some standard settings (such as on port `tcp/2376` enabled TLS). You can ensure that by SSHing to the node and verify the running processes:

```
$ docker-machine ssh node0 ps aux | grep docker
1320 root  /usr/local/bin/docker daemon -D -g /var/lib/docker -H
unix:// -H tcp://0.0.0.0:2376 --label provider=virtualbox --
tlsverify --tlscacert=/var/lib/boot2docker/ca.pem --
tlscert=/var/lib/boot2docker/server.pem --
tlskey=/var/lib/boot2docker/server-key.pem -s aufs
```

So, you can immediately this Docker daemon by, for example, starting containers and checking the Docker status:

```
                                              2. bash
darthvader:~ fsoppelsa$ docker run -ti busybox sh
Unable to find image 'busybox:latest' locally
latest: Pulling from library/busybox

385e281300cc: Pull complete
a3ed95caeb02: Pull complete
Digest: sha256:4a887a2326ec9e0fa90cce7b4764b0e627b5d6afcb81a3f73c85dc29cea00048
Status: Downloaded newer image for busybox:latest
/ # ip a
1: lo: <LOOPBACK,UP,LOWER_UP> mtu 65536 qdisc noqueue qlen 1
    link/loopback 00:00:00:00:00:00 brd 00:00:00:00:00:00
    inet 127.0.0.1/8 scope host lo
       valid_lft forever preferred_lft forever
    inet6 ::1/128 scope host
       valid_lft forever preferred_lft forever
7: eth0@if8: <BROADCAST,MULTICAST,UP,LOWER_UP,M-DOWN> mtu 1500 qdisc noqueue
    link/ether 02:42:ac:11:00:02 brd ff:ff:ff:ff:ff:ff
    inet 172.17.0.2/16 scope global eth0
       valid_lft forever preferred_lft forever
    inet6 fe80::42:acff:fe11:2/64 scope link
       valid_lft forever preferred_lft forever
/ # darthvader:~ fsoppelsa$ docker info | head -10
Containers: 1
 Running: 0
 Paused: 0
 Stopped: 1
Images: 1
Server Version: 1.11.1
Storage Driver: aufs
 Root Dir: /mnt/sda1/var/lib/docker/aufs
 Backing Filesystem: extfs
 Dirs: 4
darthvader:~ fsoppelsa$
```

Perfect! Now we provision the other three hosts, in the same exact way, by naming them `node1`, `node2`, and `node3`:

```
$ docker-machine create --driver virtualbox node1
$ docker-machine create --driver virtualbox node2
$ docker-machine create --driver virtualbox node3
```

When they finish, you will have four Docker hosts available. Check with Docker machine.

```
darthvader:~ fsoppelsa$ docker-machine ls
NAME    ACTIVE   DRIVER       STATE     URL                            SWARM   DOCKER    ERRORS
node0   *        virtualbox   Running   tcp://192.168.99.107:2376              v1.11.1
node1   -        virtualbox   Running   tcp://192.168.99.101:2376              v1.11.1
node2   -        virtualbox   Running   tcp://192.168.99.102:2376              v1.11.1
node3   -        virtualbox   Running   tcp://192.168.99.103:2376              v1.11.1
```

We're now ready to start a Swarm cluster. But, before, for this very first example in order to keep it as simple as possible, we'll go with disabling TLS for running engines. Our plan is: Run the Docker daemon on port `2375`, without TLS.

Let's make a bit of order and explain all ports combinations in detail.

Insecure	Secure
Engine: 2375	Engine: 2376
Swarm: 3375	Swarm: 3376
	Swarm v2 uses 2377 for node discovery among nodes

Port `2377` is for Swarm v2 node to discover each other nodes in the cluster.

Configuring the Docker hosts

To understand where the TLS configuration is, we'll do some exercises by turning off the TLS of all our Docker hosts. Also turning it off here is intended to motivate the readers to learn how the `swarm manage` command works by invoking it ourselves.

We have four hosts running Docker on port `tcp/2376` and with TLS, as Docker Machine creates them by default. We must reconfigure them to change the daemon port to `tls/2375` and remove TLS. So, we log in into each of them, with this command:

```
$ docker-machine ssh node0
```

Then, we gain root privileges:

```
$ sudo su -
```

And configure `boot2docker`, by modifying the file `/var/lib/boot2docker/profile`:

```
# cp /var/lib/boot2docker/profile /var/lib/boot2docker/profile-bak
# vi /var/lib/boot2docker/profile
```

We delete the rows with CACERT, SERVERKEY, and SERVERCERT and configure the daemon port to `tcp/2375` and `DOCKER_TLS` to `no`. In practice this will be our configuration:

```
EXTRA_ARGS='
--label provider=virtualbox

'
DOCKER_HOST='-H tcp://0.0.0.0:2375'
DOCKER_STORAGE=aufs
DOCKER_TLS=no
```

After this log out from the SSH session and restart the machine:

```
$ docker-machine restart node0
```

Docker is now running on port `tcp/2375` with no security. You can check this with the following command:

```
$ docker-machine ssh node0 ps aux | grep docker
 1127 root   /usr/local/bin/docker daemon -D -g /var/lib/docker -H
 unix:// -H tcp://0.0.0.0:2375 --label provider=virtualbox -s aufs
```

Finally, on your local desktop computer, unset `DOCKER_TLS_VERIFY` and re-export `DOCKER_HOST` in order to use the daemon listening on `tcp/2375` with no TLS:

```
$ unset DOCKER_TLS_VERIFY
$ export DOCKER_HOST="tcp://192.168.99.103:2375"
```

We must repeat these steps for each of our four nodes that will be part of our first Swarm.

Starting Docker Swarm

To get started with Swarm v1 (no surprise), one must pull the `swarm` image from the
Docker hub. Open the four terminals, source the environment variables for each of your
machines in each one in the first one, source node0 (`docker-machine env node0`, and
copy and paste the `env` variable to the shell), in second `node1`, and so on -, and after
completing the steps for changing the standard port and disabling TLS described some lines
above, on each of them do:

```
$ docker pull swarm
```

```
darthvader:~ fsoppelsa$ docker pull swarm
Using default tag: latest
latest: Pulling from library/swarm

51436fd4bb0d: Pull complete
c31a5390266f: Pull complete
e40019be13ea: Pull complete
a3ed95caeb02: Pull complete
Digest: sha256:3add485cb6bb71c7113243753c5f484561549d9f782154b1c809219c9754ce46
Status: Downloaded newer image for swarm:latest
```

We'll use no discovery service for the first example, but the simplest of the mechanisms,
such as the `nodes://`. With `nodes://`, the Swarm cluster nodes are connected manually,
to form a grid of peers. What the operator has to do is simply define a list of nodes IPs and
the daemon port, separated by commas, as shown:

```
nodes://192.168.99.101:2375,192.168.99.102:2375,192.168.99.103:2375,192.168
.99.107:2375
```

To use Swarm, you simply run the swarm container with some arguments. To show the help online, you type:

```
$ docker run swarm --help
```

```
darthvader:~ fsoppelsa$ docker run swarm --help
Usage: swarm [OPTIONS] COMMAND [arg...]

A Docker-native clustering system

Version: 1.2.3 (eaa53c7)

Options:
  --debug                   debug mode [$DEBUG]
  --log-level, -l "info"    Log level (options: debug, info, warn, error, fatal, panic)
  --experimental            enable experimental features
  --help, -h                show help
  --version, -v             print the version

Commands:
  create, c     Create a cluster
  list, l       List nodes in a cluster
  manage, m     Manage a docker cluster
  join, j       Join a docker cluster
  help          Shows a list of commands or help for one command

Run 'swarm COMMAND --help' for more information on a command.
```

As you see, Swarm has basically four commands:

- **Create** is used to create clusters with a discovery service, for example `token://`
- **List** shows the list of the cluster nodes
- **Manage** allows you to operate a Swarm cluster
- **Join**, in combination with a discovery service, is used for joining new nodes to an existing cluster

For now, we'll use the `manage` command. This is the command with most of the options (which you can investigate by issuing `docker run swarm manage --help`). We limit now to connect nodes. The following is the strategy on each node:

1. Expose the Swarm service through the swarm container.
2. Run this container in `daemon` (`-d`) mode.
3. Forward the standard Swarm port `tcp/3376` to the internal (on container) port `tcp/2375`.

4. Specify the list of hosts part of the cluster, with `nodes://` – each host has to be a pair `IP:port` where the port is the Docker engine port (`tcp/2375`).

So, in each terminal you're connected to every machine, execute this:

```
$ docker run \
-d \
-p 3376:2375 \
swarm manage \
nodes://192.168.99.101:2375,192.168.99.102:2375,
192.168.99.103:2375,192.168.99.107:2375
```

> When using the `nodes://` mechanism, you can use Ansible-like host range patterns, so compact the syntax of three contiguous IPs like
> nodes://192.168.99.101:2375,192.168.99.102:2375,192.168.99.103:2375
> In nodes://192.168.99.[101:103]:2375

Now, as the next step, we'll connect to it and inspect its information before starting using for running containers. For convenience, open a new terminal. We connect now not anymore to the Docker engine on one of our nodes, but to the Docker Swarm. So we will connect to `tcp/3376` and not to `tcp/2375` anymore. For the purpose of showing in detail what we're doing, let's start by sourcing `node0` variables:

```
$ docker-machine env node0
```

Copy and paste the eval line, as you already know, and check what shell variables are exported with the following command:

```
$ export | grep DOCKER_
```

We now need to do the following:

1. Change the `DOCKER_HOST` to connect to Swarm port `tcp/3376` instead of Engine `tcp/2375`
2. Disable `DOCKER_TLS_VERIFY`.
3. Disable `DOCKER_CERT_PATH`.

```
$ export DOCKER_HOST="tcp://192.168.99.107:3376"
$ unset DOCKER_TLS_VERIFY
$ unset DOCKER_CERT_PATH
```

You should have a configuration similar to this:

```
$ export | grep DOCKER
declare -x DOCKER_HOST="tcp://192.168.99.107:3376"
declare -x DOCKER_MACHINE_NAME="node0"
```

If we now connect to the Docker swarm at 3376, and show some info, we see that we're running Swarm:

Congratulations! You just started your first Docker cluster with Swarm. We can see that we still have no containers running on our cluster apart from the four swarms, but the Server Version is swarm/1.2.3, the scheduling strategy is spread, and, most importantly, we have four healthy nodes in our swarm (details of each Swarm node follow).

Also, you can get some extra information regarding the scheduler behavior of this Swarm cluster:

```
Strategy: spread
Filters: health, port, containerslots, dependency, affinity,
constraint
```

A spread scheduling strategy means that Swarm will attempt to place containers on the less utilized host and the listed filters are available when you create containers, thus allowing you to decide to manually suggest some options. For example, you might want to make your Galera cluster containers geographically near but on different hosts.

But, what's the size of this Swarm? You can see it at the very end of this output:

```
Kernel Version: 4.4.8-boot2docker
Operating System: linux
Architecture: amd64
CPUs: 4
Total Memory: 4.085 GiB
```

It means that on this tiny Swarm you have the total availability of these resources: four CPUs and 4GB of memory. That's just what we expected, by merging the computational resources of 4 VirtualBox hosts with a CPU and 1GB of memory each.

Test your Swarm cluster

Now that we have a Swarm cluster, it's time to start using it. We'll show that the spread strategy algorithm will decide to place containers to the less loaded hosts. In this example, it's really easy, as we start with four empty nodes. So, we're connected to Swarm and Swarm will put containers on hosts. We start one nginx container, mapping its port tcp/80 to the host (machine) port `tcp/80`.

```
$ docker run -d -p 80:80 nginx
2c049db55f9b093d19d575704c28ff57c4a7a1fb1937bd1c20a40cb538d7b75c
```

In this example, we see that the Swarm scheduler decided to place this container onto `node1`:

```
$ docker ps
CONTAINER ID      IMAGE              COMMAND                CREATED
  STATUS            PORTS                            NAMES
2c049db55f9b       nginx              "nginx -g 'daemon off"   About a minute ago
  Up About a minute    192.168.99.101:80->80/tcp, 443/tcp    node1/dreamy_goldberg
```

Since we have to bind a port `tcp/80` to any host, we will have only four chances, four containers on four different hosts. Let's create new nginx containers and see what happens:

```
$ docker run -d -p 80:80 nginx
577b06d592196c34ebff76072642135266f773010402ad3c1c724a0908a6997f
$ docker run -d -p 80:80 nginx
9fabe94b05f59d01dd1b6b417f48155fc2aab66d278a722855d3facc5fd7f831
$ docker run -d -p 80:80 nginx
38b44d8df70f4375eb6b76a37096f207986f325cc7a4577109ed59a771e6a66d
```

Now we have 4 nginx containers placed on our 4 Swarm hosts:

```
$ docker ps --format "{{.ID}}: {{.Ports}} {{.Command}}"
38b44d8df70f: 192.168.99.103:80->80/tcp, 443/tcp "nginx -g 'daemon off"
9fabe94b05f5: 192.168.99.102:80->80/tcp, 443/tcp "nginx -g 'daemon off"
577b06d59219: 192.168.99.107:80->80/tcp, 443/tcp "nginx -g 'daemon off"
2c049db55f9b: 192.168.99.101:80->80/tcp, 443/tcp "nginx -g 'daemon off"
```

Now we try to create a new nginx:

```
$ docker run -d -p 80:80 nginx
docker: Error response from daemon: Unable to find a node that
satisfies the following conditions
[port 80 (Bridge mode)].
See 'docker run --help'.
```

What happened is just that Swarm wasn't able to find a suitable host to place a new container on, because on all hosts, port `tcp/80` are all occupied. After running these 4 nginx containers, plus the four swarm containers (for the infrastructure management), as we expected, we have eight running containers on this Swarm cluster:

```
$ docker info
Containers: 8
 Running: 8
 Paused: 0
 Stopped: 0
```

This is how Swarm v1 was intended to work (and still does its job).

Swarm, today

In this section, we'll set up a small cluster with the new Swarm mode built in Docker Engine 1.12 or later.

At the DockerCon16, among the big announcements, two drew big attention regarding containers orchestration:

- The integration between the Engine and Swarm, called the Docker Swarm mode.
- SwarmKit

In practice, the Docker daemon, starting from version 1.12, adds the possibility to run a so-called Swarm Mode. New CLI commands were added to the docker client, such as `node`, `service`, `stack`, `deploy`, alongside with, of course, `swarm`.

We'll cover Swarm Mode and SwarmKit in more detail starting from `Chapter 3`, *Meeting Docker Swarm Mode*, but now that we finished the example with Swarm v1, we're going to give the reader a taste on how Swarm v2 has a much simpler user experience than v1. The only requirement to use Swarm v2 is to have a daemon version of at least version 1.12-rc1. But with Docker Machine 0.8.0-rc1+, you can provision Docker hosts fulfilling this requirement with the usual procedure.

Docker also announced Docker for AWS and Docker for Azure at DockerCon 2016. Not only AWS and Azure, but actually we're also fans of DigitalOcean, so we created a new tool that wraps around `doctl` the DigitalOcean command line interface, to help provision Docker cluster in the new massively way. The tool is called `belt` and now available from `http://github.com/chanwit/belt`. You can pull belt with this command:

```
go get github.com/chanwit/belt
```

or download the binary from the **Release** tab of the project.

First, we'll prepare a template file for provisioning on DigitalOcean. Your `.belt.yaml` will look like this:

```
$ cat .belt.yaml
---
digitalocean:
  region: sgp1
  image: 18153887
  ssh_user: root
  ssh_key_fingerprint: 816630
```

Please note that my image number 18153887 is the snapshot containing Docker 1.12. DigitalOcean usually makes the latest Docker image available after every release. To make you able to control your cluster, SSH key needs to be there. For the field ssh_key_fingerprint, you can either put the finger print as well as the key ID.

Do not forget to set your DIGITALOCEAN_ACCESS_TOKEN environment variable. Also, Belt recognizes the same set of Docker Machine shell variables. If you are familiar with Docker Machine you'll know how to set them. To refresh, these are the shell variables we introduced in the previous section:

- export DOCKER_TLS_VERIFY="1"
- export DOCKER_HOST="tcp://<IP ADDRESS>:2376"
- export DOCKER_CERT_PATH="/Users/user/.docker/machine/machines/machine"
- export DOCKER_MACHINE_NAME="machine"

So, now let's see how to use Belt:

```
$ export DIGITALOCEAN_ACCESS_TOKEN=1b207 .. snip .. b6581c
```

Now we create a Swarm of four nodes each with 512M of memory:

```
$ belt create 512mb node[1:4]
ID              Name      Public IPv4      Memory  VCPUs  Disk
18511682        node1                      512     1      20
18511683        node4                      512     1      20
18511684        node3                      512     1      20
18511681        node2                      512     1      20
```

You can see that we can specify a set of nodes with similar syntax node[1:4]. This command created four nodes on DigitalOcean. Please wait for about 55 seconds for all nodes to be provisioned. Then you can list them:

```
$ belt ls
ID              Name      Public IPv4       Status   Tags
18511681        node2     128.199.105.119   active
18511682        node1     188.166.183.86    active
18511683        node4     188.166.183.103   active
18511684        node3     188.166.183.157   active
```

Their status now has changed from "new" to "active". All IP addresses are assigned. Everything is good to go for now.

We now can start Swarm.

Before that make sure we are running Docker 1.12. We check this on `node1`.

```
$ belt active node1
node1
$ belt docker version
Client:
 Version:      1.12.0-rc2
 API version:  1.24
 Go version:   go1.6.2
 Git commit:   906eacd
 Built:        Fri Jun 17 21:02:41 2016
 OS/Arch:      linux/amd64
 Experimental: true
Server:
 Version:      1.12.0-rc2
 API version:  1.24
 Go version:   go1.6.2
 Git commit:   906eacd
 Built:        Fri Jun 17 21:02:41 2016
 OS/Arch:      linux/amd64
 Experimental: true
```

The `belt docker` command is just a thin wrapper command that sends the whole command line going through SSH to your Docker host. So this tool will not get in the way and your Docker Engines is always in-control.

Now we will initialize the first node with Swarm Mode.

```
$ belt docker swarm init
Swarm initialized: current node (c0llmsc5t1tsbtcblrx6ji1ty) is now
a manager.
```

Then we'll join other three nodes to this newly formed cluster. Joining a large cluster is a tedious task. Instead of going through every node and do docker swarm join manually, we'll let `belt` do this for us:

```
$ belt swarm join node1 node[2:4]
node3: This node joined a Swarm as a worker.
node2: This node joined a Swarm as a worker.
node4: This node joined a Swarm as a worker.
```

You can of course be able to run: `belt --host node2 docker swarm join <node1's IP>:2377` to manually join node2 to your cluster.

And you'll get this view of cluster:

```
$ belt docker node ls
ID               NAME    MEMBERSHIP   STATUS   AVAILABILITY   MANAGER STATUS
4m5479vud9qc6qs7wuy3krr4u    node2   Accepted     Ready    Active
4mkw7ccwep8pez1jfeok6su2o    node4   Accepted     Ready    Active
a395rnht2p754w1beh74bf7f1    node3   Accepted     Ready    Active
c011msc5t1tsbtcblrx6ji1ty *  node1   Accepted     Ready    Active
Leader
```

Congratulations! You just installed a Swarm cluster on DigitalOcean.

We now create a service for `nginx`. This command creates an Nginx service with 2 instances of containers published at port 80.

```
$ belt docker service create --name nginx --replicas 2 -p 80:80
nginx
d5qmntf1tvvztw9r9bhx1hokd
```

Here we go:

```
$ belt docker service ls
ID               NAME    REPLICAS   IMAGE    COMMAND
d5qmntf1tvvz    nginx   2/2        nginx
```

Now let's scale it to 4 nodes.

```
$ belt docker service scale nginx=4
nginx scaled to 4
$ belt docker service ls
ID              NAME    REPLICAS  IMAGE   COMMAND
d5qmntf1tvvz    nginx   4/4       nginx
```

Similar to Docker Swarm, you can now use `belt ip` to see where the node runs. You can use any IP address to browse the NGINX service. It's available on every node.

```
$ belt ip node2
128.199.105.119
```

This is how Swarm Mode looks like starting from Docker 1.12.

Summary

In this chapter, we met Docker Swarm, defined its aims, features, and architecture. We also reviewed some of the other possible open source alternatives to Swarm, and their relationships with it. Finally, we installed and started using Swarm by creating a simple local cluster made of four hosts on Virtualbox and on Digital Ocean.

Clusterize containers with Swarm will be the main topic for the whole book, but before we start using Swarm in production, we'll understand some theory before, beginning with the discovery services, the topic of `Chapter 2`, *Discover the Discovery Services*.

2
Discover the Discovery Services

In `Chapter 1`, *Welcome to Docker Swarm* we created a simple yet well functioning local Docker Swarm cluster using the `nodes://` mechanism. This system is not very practical, except for learning the Swarm fundamentals.

In fact, it is just a flat model that does not contemplate any true master-slave architecture, not to mention the high-level services, such as nodes discovery and auto-configuration, resilience, leader elections, and failover (high availability). In practice, it's not suitable for a production environment.

Apart from `nodes://`, Swarm v1 officially supports four discovery services; however, one of them, Token, is a trivial non-production one. Basically, with Swarm v1 you need to integrate a discovery service manually, while with Swarm Mode (from Docker 1.12), a discovery service, Etcd, is already integrated. In this chapter we're going to cover:

- Discovery services
- A test-grade discovery service: Token
- Raft theory and Etcd
- Zookeeper and Consul

Before exploring these services in depth, lets us discuss what is a discovery service?

A discovery service

Imagine you're running a Swarm cluster on a static configuration, similar to the one in `Chapter 1`, *Welcome to Docker Swarm*, networking is flat and every container is assigned a specific task, for example a MySQL database. It's easy to locate the MySQL container because you assigned it a defined IP address or you run some DNS server. It's easy to notify whether this single container is working or not and it's a known fact that it won't change its port (`tcp/3336`). Moreover, it's not necessary that our MySQL container announces its availability as a database container with its IP and port: We, of course, already know that.

This is the pet model, mocked-up manually by a system administrator. However, since we're more advanced operators, we want to drive a cattle instead.

So, imagine you're running a Swarm made of hundreds of nodes, hosting several applications running a certain number of services (web servers, databases, key-value stores, caches, and queues). These applications run on a massive number of containers that may dynamically change their IP address, either because you restart them, you create new ones, you spin up replicas, or some high availability mechanism starts new ones for you.

How can you find the MySQL services acting of your Acme app? How do you ensure that your load balancer knows the address of your 100 Nginx frontends so that their functionalities don't break? How do you notify if a service has moved away with a different configuration?

You use a discovery service.

A so called discovery service is a mechanism with many features. There are different services you can choose from, with more or less similar qualities, with their pros and their cons, but basically all discovery services target distributed systems, hence they must be distributed on all cluster nodes, be scalable, and fault-tolerant. The main goal of a discovery service is to help services to find and talk to one another. In order to do that, they need to save (register) information related to where each service is located, by announcing themselves, and they usually do that by acting as a key-value store. Discovery services existed way before of the rise of Docker, but the problem has become a lot more difficult with the advent of containers and container orchestration.

Summarizing again, through a discovery service:

- You can locate single services in the infrastructure
- You can notify a service configuration change
- Services register their availability
- And more

Typically, a discovery service is made as a key-value store. Docker Swarm v1, officially, supports the following discovery services. However, you can integrate your own using `libkv` abstraction interface, you can integrate your own one as shown in the following site:

`https://github.com/docker/docker/tree/master/pkg/discovery`.

- Token
- Consul 0.5.1+
- Etcd 2.0+
- ZooKeeper 3.4.5+

However, the Etcd library has been integrated into the Swarm mode as its built-in discovery service.

Token

Docker Swarm v1 includes an out-of-the-box discovery service, called Token. Token is integrated into the Docker Hub; hence, it requires all the Swarm nodes to be connected to the Internet and able to reach the Docker Hub. This is the main limitation of Token but, you will soon see, Token will allow us to make some practice in handling clusters.

In a nutshell, Token requires you to generate a UUID called, in fact, token. With this UUID, you can create a manager, act like a master, and join slaves to the cluster.

Re-architecting the example of Chapter 1 with token

If we want to keep it practical, it's time to take a look at an example. We'll use token to re-architect the example of `Chapter 1`, *Welcome to Docker Swarm*. As a novelty, the cluster will be not flat anymore, but it will consist of 1 master and 3 slaves and each node will have security enabled by default.

The master node will be the node exposing Swarm port 3376. We'll connect specifically to it in order to be able to drive the entire cluster.

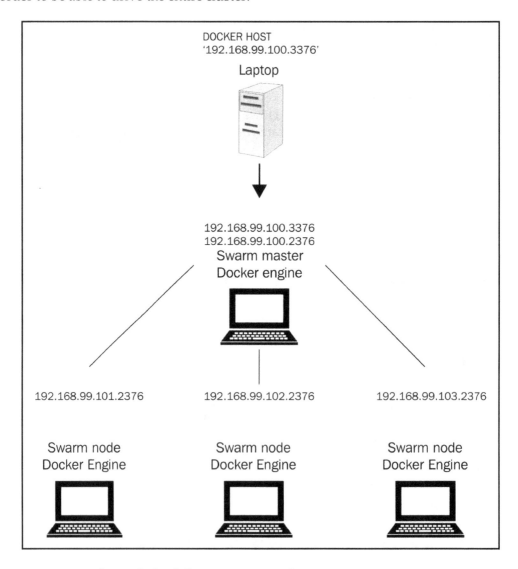

We can create 4 nodes with the following command:

```
$ for i in `seq 0 3`; do docker-machine create -d virtualbox
node$i;
done
```

Now, we have four machines running the last version of the Engine, with the TLS enabled. This means, as you remember, that the Engine is exposing port 2376 and not 2375.

```
$ docker-machine ls
NAME     ACTIVE   DRIVER       STATE     URL                            SWARM   DOCKER
node0    -        virtualbox   Running   tcp://192.168.99.100:2376              v1.11.2
node1    -        virtualbox   Running   tcp://192.168.99.101:2376              v1.11.2
node2    -        virtualbox   Running   tcp://192.168.99.102:2376              v1.11.2
node3    -        virtualbox   Running   tcp://192.168.99.103:2376              v1.11.2
```

We will now create the cluster, starting from the master. Pick up one of the nodes, for example node0, and source its variables:

```
$ eval $(docker-machine env node0)
```

We now generate the cluster token and the unique ID. For this purpose, we use the swarm create command:

```
$ docker run swarm create
3b905f46fef903800d51513d51acbbbe
```

```
$ eval $(docker-machine env node0)
$ docker run swarm create
Unable to find image 'swarm:latest' locally
latest: Pulling from library/swarm

1e61bbec5d24: Pull complete
8c7b2f6b74da: Pull complete
245a8db4f1e1: Pull complete
Digest: sha256:661f2e4c9470e7f6238cebf603bcf5700c8b948894ac9e35f2cf6f63dcda723a
Status: Downloaded newer image for swarm:latest
3b905f46fef903800d51513d51acbbbe
```

As a result, the swarm container outputs the token, and the protocol that we'll be using in this example will be invoked as shown: token://3b905f46fef903800d51513d51acbbbe

Take note of this token ID, for example assigning it to a shell variable:

```
$ TOKEN=3b905f46fef903800d51513d51acbbbe
```

We now create a master and try to meet, at least, some of the basic standard security requirements, how is, we'll enable TLS encryption. As we'll see in a moment, the `swarm` command accepts TLS options as arguments. But how do we pass keys and certificates to a container? For this, we'll use the certificates generated by Docker Machine and placed in `/var/lib/boot2docker` on the host.

In practice, we mount a volume from the Docker host to the container on the Docker host. All remotely and controlled thanks to the environment variables.

With the `node0` variables already sourced, we start the Swarm master with the following command:

```
$ docker run -ti -v /var/lib/boot2docker:/certs -p 3376:3376 swarm
manage -H 0.0.0.0:3376 -tls --tlscacert=/certs/ca.pem --
tlscert=/certs/server.pem --tlskey=/certs/server-key.pem
token://$TOKEN
```

To begin, we run the container in an interactive mode to observe the swarm output. Then, we mount the node `/var/lib/boot2docker` directory to the `/certs` directory inside the swarm container. We redirect the `3376` Swarm secure ports from node0 to the swarm container. We execute the `swarm` command in the manage mode by binding it to `0.0.0.0:3376`. Then we specify some certificates options and file paths and finally describe that the discovery service in use is token, with our token.

```
$ eval $(docker-machine env node0)
$ docker run -ti -v /var/lib/boot2docker:/certs -p 3376:3376 swarm manage -H 0.0.0.0:3376 -tls --tlscacert=/certs/
ca.pem --tlscert=/certs/server.pem --tlskey=/certs/server-key.pem token://$TOKEN
INFO[0000] Listening for HTTP                        addr=0.0.0.0:3376 proto=tcp
INFO[0001] Registered Engine node0 at 192.168.99.100:2376
```

With this node running, let's open another terminal and join a node to this Swarm. Let's start by sourcing the `node1` variables. Now, we need swarm to use the `join` command, in order to join the cluster whose master is `node0`:

```
$ docker run -d swarm join --addr=192.168.99.101:2376
token://$TOKEN
```

Here we specify the host (itself) at address `192.168.99.101` to join the cluster.

```
$ eval $(docker-machine env node1)
$ export | grep DOCKER_HOST
declare -x DOCKER_HOST="tcp://192.168.99.101:2376"
$ docker run -ti swarm join --addr=192.168.99.101:2376 token://$TOKEN
INFO[0000] Registering on the discovery service every 1m0s...   addr=192.168.99.101:2376 discovery=token://3b905f46
fef903800d51513d51acbbbe
```

If we jump back to the first terminal, we'll see that the master has noticed that a node has joined the cluster. So, at this point of time we have a Swarm cluster composed of one master and one slave.

```
INFO[0180] Registered Engine node1 at 192.168.99.101:2376
```

Since we now understand the mechanism, we can stop both the `docker` commands in the terminals and rerun them with the `-d` option. So, to run containers in daemon mode:

Master:

```
$ docker run -t-d -v /var/lib/boot2docker:/certs -p 3376:3376 swarm
manage -H 0.0.0.0:3376 -tls --tlscacert=/certs/ca.pem --
tlscert=/certs/server.pem --tlskey=/certs/server-key.pem
token://$TOKEN
```

Node:

```
$ docker run -d swarm join --addr=192.168.99.101:2376
token://$TOKEN
```

We will now proceed by joining the other two nodes to the cluster, source their variables, and repeat the last command as shown:

```
$ eval $(docker-machine env node2)
$ docker run -d swarm join --addr=192.168.99.102:2376
token://$TOKEN
$ eval $(docker-machine env node3)
$ docker run -d swarm join --addr=192.168.99.103:2376
token://$TOKEN
```

For example, if we open a third terminal, source the `node0` variables, and specifically connect to port `3376` (Swarm) instead of `2376` (Docker Engine), we can see some fancy output coming from the `docker info` command. For example, there are three nodes in a cluster:

```
$ docker info | egrep "^Node|node"
Nodes: 3
 node1: 192.168.99.101:2376
 node2: 192.168.99.102:2376
 node3: 192.168.99.103:2376
WARNING: No kernel memory limit support
$ 
```

So, we have created a cluster with one master, three slaves, and with TLS enabled and ready to accept containers.

We can ensure that from the master and list the nodes in the cluster. We will now use the `swarm list` command:

```
$ docker run swarm list token://$TOKEN
```

```
$ docker run swarm list token://$TOKEN
192.168.99.103:2376
192.168.99.102:2376
192.168.99.101:2376
```

Token limitations

Token is not deprecated yet, but probably it will be deprecated very soon. The standard requirement that every node in the Swarm should have internet connectivity is not very convenient. Moreover, the access to the Docker Hub makes this technique depend on Hub availability. In practice, it has the Hub as a single point of failure. However, using token, we were able to understand what's behind the scenes a little bit better and we met the Swarm v1 commands: `create`, `manage`, `join`, and `list`.

Now it's time to proceed further and get acquainted with real discovery services and the consensus algorithm, a cardinal principle in fault-tolerant systems.

Raft

Consensus is an algorithm in distributed systems that forces agents in the system to agree on consistent values and elect a leader.

Some well-known consensus algorithms are Paxos and Raft. Paxos and Raft deliver similar performances but Raft is less complex, easier to understand, and therefore becoming very popular in distributed store implementations.

As consensus algorithms, Consul and Etcd implement Raft while ZooKeeper implements Paxos. The CoreOS Etcd Go library, implementing Raft, is included into SwarmKit and Swarm Mode as a dependency (in `vendor/`), so in this book we'll focus more on it.

Raft is described in detail in the Ongaro, Ousterhout paper, and it is available at `https://r amcloud.stanford.edu/raft.pdf`. In the upcoming section we'll summarize its basic concepts.

Raft theory

Raft was designed with simplicity in mind and compared to Paxos, it truly achieves this goal (there are even academic publications demonstrating this). For our purpose, the main difference between Raft and Paxos is that in Raft, messages and logs are sent only by the cluster leader to its peers, making the algorithm more understandable and easier to implement. The sample library that we'll use, in the theory section, is the Go one delivered by CoreOS Etcd, available at `https://github.com/coreos/etcd/tree/master/raft`.

A Raft cluster is made of nodes that must maintain a replicated state machine in a consistent manner, no matter what: new nodes can join, old nodes can crash or become unavailable, but this state machine must be kept in sync.

To achieve this failure-aware goal, typically Raft clusters consist of an odd number of nodes, such as three or five to avoid split-brains. A split-brain occurs when the remaining node(s) split themselves in groups that can't agree on a leader election. If there is an odd number of nodes, they can finally agree on a leader with a majority. With an even number, the election can close with a 50%-50% result, which should not happen.

Back to Raft, a Raft cluster is defined as a type raft struct in `raft.go` and includes information such as the leader UUID, the current term, a pointer to the log, and utilities to check the status of quorum and elections. Let's illustrate all these concepts step-by-step by decomposing the definition of the cluster component, a Node. A Node is defined as an interface in `node.go`, which is implemented canonically in this library as a `type node struct`.

```
type Node interface {
    Tick()
    Campaign(ctx context.Context) error
    Propose(ctx context.Context, data []byte) error
    ProposeConfChange(ctx context.Context, cc pb.ConfChange) error
    Step(ctx context.Context, msg pb.Message) error
    Ready() <-chan Ready
    Advance()
    ApplyConfChange(cc pb.ConfChange) *pb.ConfState
    Status() Status
    ReportUnreachable(id uint64)
    ReportSnapshot(id uint64, status SnapshotStatus)
    Stop()
}
```

Every node keeps a tick (incremented by `Tick()`), denoting the term or period of time or epoch, of an arbitrary length, which is the current running instant. At every term, a node can be in one of the following StateType:

- Leader
- Candidate
- Follower

Under normal conditions, there is only one leader and all other nodes are followers. The leader, in order to make us respect its authority, sends heartbeat messages to its followers at regular intervals. When followers note that heartbeat messages are not arriving any longer, they understand that the leader is not available anymore and therefore they increment their values and become candidates and then attempt to become a leader by running `Campaign()`. They start with voting for themselves and trying to reach a quorum. When a node achieves this, a new leader is elected.

`Propose()` is a method of proposal to append data to the log. A log is the data structure used in Raft to synchronize the cluster status and it's another crucial concept in Etcd. It's saved in a stable storage (memory), which has the ability to compact the log when it becomes huge to save space (snapshotting). The leader ensures that log is always in a consistent state and commits new data to append to its log (a master-log) only when it's sure that this information has been replicated through the majority of its followers, so there is an agreement. There is a `Step()` method, which advances the state machine to the next step.

`ProposeConfChange()` is a method that allows us to change the cluster configuration at runtime. It is demonstrated to be safe under any condition, thanks to its two-phase mechanism that ensures that there is an agreement on this change from every possible majority. `ApplyConfChange()` applies this change to the current node.

Then there is `Ready()`. In the Node interface, this function returns a read-only channel that returns encapsulated specification of messages that are ready to be read, saved to storage, and committed. Usually, after invoking Ready and applying its entries, a client must call `Advance()`, to notify that a progress in Ready has been made. In practice, `Ready()` and `Advance()` are parts of the method through which Raft keeps a high level of coherency, by avoiding inconsistencies in the log, its content, and status synchronization.

This is how Raft implementation looks like in CoreOS' Etcd.

Raft in practice

If you want to put your hands and practice Raft, a good idea is to use the `raftexample` from Etcd and start a three-member cluster.

Since Docker Compose YAML files are self-describing, the following example is of a compose file ready to be run:

```
version: '2'
services:
  raftexample1:
      image: fsoppelsa/raftexample
      command: --id 1 --cluster
      http://127.0.0.1:9021,http://127.0.0.1:9022,
      http://127.0.0.1:9023 --port 9121
      ports:
        - "9021:9021"
        - "9121:9121"
  raftexample2:
      image: fsoppelsa/raftexample
```

```
        command: --id 2 --cluster
        http://127.0.0.1:9021,http://127.0.0.1:9022,
        http://127.0.0.1:9023 --port 9122
        ports:
          - "9022:9022"
          - "9122:9122"
    raftexample3:
        image: fsoppelsa/raftexample
        command: --id 3 --cluster
        http://127.0.0.1:9021,http://127.0.0.1:9022,
        http://127.0.0.1:9023 --port 9123
        ports:
          - "9023:9023"
          - "9123:9123"
```

This template creates three Raft services (`raftexample1`, `raftexample2`, and `raftexample3`). Each runs an instance of raftexample, by exposing the APIs with `--port` and using a static cluster configuration with `--cluster`.

You can start this on a Docker host with:

```
docker-compose -f raftexample.yaml up
```

Now you can play, for example by killing the leader, observe new elections, set some values via API to one of the containers, remove the container, update the value, restart the container, retrieve this value, and note that it was correctly upgraded.

Interactions with the APIs can be done via curl, as described at `https://github.com/coreos/etcd/tree/master/contrib/raftexample`:

```
curl -L http://127.0.0.1:9121/testkey -XPUT -d value
curl -L http://127.0.0.1:9121/testkey
```

We leave this exercise to the more enthusiastic readers.

 When you're trying to adopt a Raft implementation, choose Etcd's Raft library for highest performance and choose Consul (from Serf library) for ready-to-use and easier implementation.

Etcd

Etcd is a highly available, distributed, and consistent key-value store that is used for shared configuration and service discovery. Some notable projects that use Etcd are SwarmKit, Kubernetes, and Fleet.

Etcd can gracefully manage master elections in case of network splits and can tolerate node failure, including the master. Applications, in our case Docker containers and Swarm nodes, can read and write data into Etcd's key-value storage, for example the location of services.

Re architecting the example of Chapter 1 with Etcd

We once again create an example with one manager and three nodes, this time by illustrating Etcd.

This time, we'll need a real discovery service. We can simulate a non-HA system by running the Etcd server inside Docker itself. We create a cluster made of four hosts, with the following names:

- `etcd-m` will be the Swarm master and will host also the Etcd server
- `etcd-1`: The first Swarm node
- `etcd-2`: The second Swarm node
- `etcd-3`: The third Swarm node

The operator, by connecting to `etcd-m:3376`, will operate Swarm on the three nodes, as usual.

Let's start by creating the hosts with Machine:

```
for i in m `seq 1 3`; do docker-machine create -d virtualbox etcd-$i;
done
```

Now we will run the Etcd master on `etcd-m`. We use the `quay.io/coreos/etcd` official image from CoreOS, following the documentation available at `https://github.com/coreos/etcd/blob/master/Documentation/op-guide/clustering.md`.

First, in a terminal, we source the `etcd-m` shell variables:

```
term0$ eval $(docker-machine env etcd-m)
```

Then, we run the Etcd master in a single-host mode (that is, no fault-tolerance, and so on):

```
docker run -d -p 2379:2379 -p 2380:2380 -p 4001:4001 \
--name etcd quay.io/coreos/etcd \
-name etcd-m -initial-advertise-peer-urls http://$(docker-machine
ip etcd-m):2380 \
-listen-peer-urls http://0.0.0.0:2380 \
-listen-client-urls http://0.0.0.0:2379,http://0.0.0.0:4001 \
-advertise-client-urls http://$(docker-machine ip etcd-m):2379 \
-initial-cluster-token etcd-cluster-1 \
-initial-cluster etcd-m=http://$(docker-machine ip etcd-m):2380
-initial-cluster-state new
```

What we do here is start the Etcd image in the daemon (-d) mode and expose ports 2379 (Etcd client communication), 2380 (Etcd server communication), 4001 (), and specify the following Etcd options:

- `name`: The name of the node, in this case we select etcd-m, as the name of the node hosting this container
- `initial-advertise-peer-urls` in this static configuration is the address:port of the cluster
- `listen-peer-urls`
- `listen-client-urls`
- `advertise-client-urls`
- `initial-cluster-token`
- `initial-cluster`
- `initial-cluster-state`

We can ensure that this one-node Etcd cluster is healthy, using the `etcdctl cluster-health` command-line utility:

```
term0$ docker run fsoppelsa/etcdctl -C $(dm ip etcd-m):2379
cluster-health
```

```
$ docker run fsoppelsa/etcdctl \
> -C $(docker-machine ip etcdm):2379 \
> cluster-health

cluster is healthy
member e31763b19431cae7 is healthy
```

This indicates that Etcd is at least up and running, so we can use it to set up a Swarm v1 cluster.

We create the Swarm manager on the same etcd-m host:

```
term0$ docker run -d -p 3376:3376 swarm manage \
-H tcp://0.0.0.0:3376 \`
etcd://$(docker-machine ip etcd-m)/swarm
```

This exposes the usual 3376 port from host to container, but this time starts the manager using the etcd:// URL for the discovery service.

We now join the nodes, etcd-1, etcd-2, and etcd-3.

As usual, we can source and command machines, one, for each terminal:

```
term1$ eval $(docker-machine env etcd-1)
term1$ docker run -d swarm join --advertise \
$(docker-machine ip etcd-1):2379 \
etcd://$(docker-machine ip etcd-m):2379
term2$ eval $(docker-machine env etcd-2)
term1$ docker run -d swarm join --advertise \
$(docker-machine ip etcd-2):2379 \
etcd://$(docker-machine ip etcd-m):2379
term3$ eval $(docker-machine env etcd-3)
term3$ docker run -d swarm join --advertise \
$(docker-machine ip etcd-3):2379 \
etcd://$(docker-machine ip etcd-m):2379
```

With join -advertise, we order the local node to join the Swarm cluster, using the Etcd service running and exposed on etcd-m.

We now go to etcd-m and see the nodes of our cluster, by invoking the Etcd discovery service:

```
$ docker run swarm list etcd://$(docker-machine ip etcdm):2379
time="2016-06-29T19:51:31Z" level=info msg="Initializing discovery without TLS"
192.168.99.106:2379
192.168.99.107:2379
192.168.99.109:2379
```

We have the three hosts already joined to the cluster as expected.

ZooKeeper

ZooKeeper is another widely used and high-performance coordination service for distributed applications. Apache ZooKeeper was originally a subproject of Hadoop but is now a top-level project. It is a highly consistent, scalable, and reliable key-value store that can be used as a discovery service for a Docker Swarm v1 cluster. As mentioned previously, ZooKeeper uses Paxos, rather than Raft.

Similar to Etcd, when ZooKeeper forms a nodes cluster with a quorum, it has one leader and the remaining nodes are followers. Internally, ZooKeeper uses its own ZAB, ZooKeeper Broadcasting Protocol, to maintain consistency and integrity.

Consul

The last discovery service we're going to see here is Consul, a tool for discovering and configuring services. It provides an API that allows clients to register and discover services. Similar to Etcd and ZooKeeper, Consul is a key-value store with a REST API. It can perform health checks to determine service availability and uses the Raft consensus algorithm via the Serf library. Similar to Etcd and Zookeeper, of course, Consul can form a high availability quorum with leader election. Its member management system is based on `memberlist`, an efficient Gossip protocol implementation.

Re architecting the example of Chapter 1 with Consul

We will now create another Swarm v1, but in this section we create machines on a cloud provider, DigitalOcean. To do so, you need an access token. However, if you don't have a DigitalOcean account, you can replace `--driver digitalocean` with `--driver virtualbox` and run this example locally.

Let's start by creating the Consul master:

```
$ docker-machine create --driver digitalocean consul-m
$ eval $(docker-machine env consul-m)
```

We start the first agent here. Although we call it an agent, we are actually going to run it in the Server mode. We use the server mode (-server) and make it into the bootstrap node (-bootstrap). With these options, Consul will not perform the leader selection as it will force itself to be the leader.

```
$ docker run -d --name=consul --net=host \
consul agent \
-client=$(docker-machine ip consul-m) \
-bind=$(docker-machine ip consul-m) \
-server -bootstrap
```

In case of a quorum for HA, the second and the third must be start with -botstrap-expect 3 to allow them to form a high availability cluster.

Now, we can use curl command to test if our Consul quorum started successfully.

```
$ curl -X GET http://$(docker-machine ip consul-m):8500/v1/kv/
```

If it's silent without showing any error, then Consul works correctly.

Next, we're going to create another three nodes on DigitalOcean.

```
$ for i in `seq 1 3`; do docker-machine create -d digitalocean
consul-$i;
done
```

Let's start the master and use Consul as a discovery mechanism:

```
$ eval $(docker-machine env consul-m)
$ docker run -d -p 3376:3376 swarm manage \
-H tcp://0.0.0.0:3376 \
consul://$(docker-machine ip consul-m):8500/swarm
$ eval $(docker-machine env consul-1)
$ docker run -d swarm join \
  --advertise $(docker-machine ip consul-1):2376 \
  consul://$(docker-machine ip consul-m):8500/swarm
$ eval $(docker-machine env consul-2)
$ docker run -d swarm join \
  --advertise $(docker-machine ip consul-2):2376 \
  consul://$(docker-machine ip consul-m):8500/swarm
$ eval $(docker-machine env consul-3)
$ docker run -d swarm join \
  --advertise $(docker-machine ip consul-3):2376 \
  consul://$(docker-machine ip consul-m):8500/swarm
```

Here's what we get when running the `swarm list` command: All nodes joined the Swarm, so the example is running.

```
$ docker run swarm list consul://$(docker-machine ip consul-m):8500/swarm
time="2016-07-01T21:45:18Z" level=info msg="Initializing discovery without TLS"
    104.131.101.173:2376
    104.131.63.75:2376
    104.236.56.53:2376
```

Towards a decentralized discovery service

The limitation of a Swarm v1 architecture is that it uses a centralized and external discovery service. This approach makes every agent to talk to the external discovery service and the discovery service servers may see their load growing exponentially. From our experiments, for a 500-node cluster, we recommend to form an HA discovery service with at least three machines with medium-high specification, say 8 cores with 8 GB of RAM.

To properly address this problem, the discovery service used by SwarmKit and by Swarm Mode has been designed with decentralization in mind. Swarm mode uses the same discovery service codebase, Etcd, on all nodes, with no single point of failure.

Summary

In this chapter, we got familiar with the concept of consensus and discovery service. We understood that they play an essential role in orchestration clusters, as they provide services such as fault-tolerance and safe configurations. We analyzed a consensus algorithm, such as Raft in detail, before looking to two concrete Raft discovery services implementations, Etcd and Consul, putting things in practice and re-architecting basic examples with them. In the next chapter we're now going to start exploring SwarmKit and Swarm that use the embedded Etcd library.

3
Meeting Docker Swarm Mode

At Dockercon 16, the Docker team presented a new way of operating Swarm clusters, called Swarm Mode. The announcement was slightly anticipated by the introduction of a new set of tools, said to *operate distributed systems at any scale* called **Swarmkit**.

In this chapter, we will:

- Introduce Swarmkit
- Introduce Swarm Mode
- Compare Swarm v1, Swarmkit, and Swarm Mode
- Create a test Swarmkit cluster, and launch services on it

Do not skip reading the Swarmkit section, because Swarmkit acts as a foundation for Swarm mode. Seeing Swarmkit is the way we chose to introduce Swarm Mode concepts, such as nodes, services, tasks.

We'll show how to create production-level big Swarm Mode clusters in `Chapter 4`, *Creating a Production-Grade Swarm*.

Swarmkit

Alongside with Swarm Mode, the Docker team at DockerCon16 released Swarmkit, defined as a:

> *"Toolkit for orchestrating distributed systems at any scale. It includes primitives for node discovery, raft-based consensus, task scheduling, and more."*

Swarms clusters are made of active nodes, that can either act as managers or workers.

Managers, that coordinate via Raft (that is, they elect leaders when quorum is available, as described in Chapter 2, *Discover the Discovery Services*), are responsible for allocating resources, orchestrating services, and dispatching tasks along the cluster. Workers run tasks.

The cluster goal is to execute *services*, so what's required to be run is defined at high level. For example, a service could be "web". Work units assigned to nodes are instead called **tasks**. A task allocated for a "web" service could be, for example, a container running the nginx container, and may be named as web.5.

It's very important to notice that we are speaking of services and that a service may be containers. May be, it's not necessary. In this book, our focus will be of course on containers, but the intention of Swarmkit is to theoretically abstract orchestration of any object.

Versions and support

A note on versions. Docker Swarm mode, which we'll introduce in the upcoming sections, is compatible only with Docker 1.12+. With Swarmkit, instead, you can orchestrate even previous versions of Docker Engines, for example, 1.11 or 1.10.

Swarmkit architecture

Swarmkit is the orchestration mechanism released to handle clusters of services of any size.

In a Swarmkit cluster, nodes can be either **managers** (of the cluster) or **workers** (the workhorses of cluster, nodes that execute compute operations).

There should be an odd number of managers, preferably 3 or 5, so that if there will be no split brains (as explained in Chapter 2, *Discover the Discovery Services*), and a majority of managers will drive the cluster. A quorum is always required by the Raft consensus algorithm.

A Swarmkit cluster can host any arbitrary number of workers: 1, 10, 100, or 2,000.

On managers, **services** may be defined and load balanced. For example, a service may be "web". A "web" service will be physically made of several **tasks**, running on the cluster nodes, including the managers, for example, one task can be a single nginx Docker container.

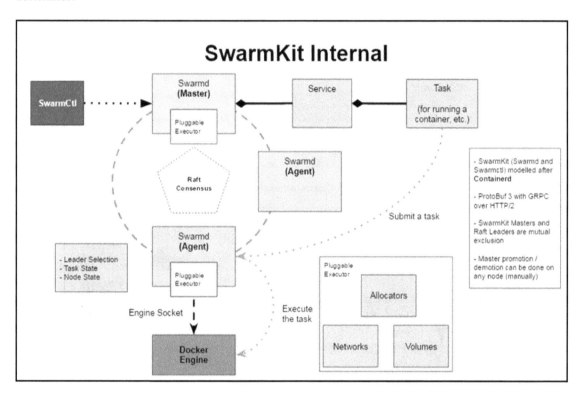

In Swarmkit, an operator uses a **Swarmctl** binary to interact with the system remotely, invoking operations on the leader master. Masters, that run a binary called **Swarmd**, agree on a leader via Raft, keep the status of services and tasks, and schedule jobs on workers.

Workers run the Docker Engine, and take jobs running them as separate containers.

The Swarmkit architecture can be subject to a redraw, but the core components (masters and workers) are going to stay. Rather, new objects can possibly be added with plugins, for allocating resources such as networks and volumes.

How a manager chooses the best node for a task

The way that Swarmkit spawns tasks over the cluster is called **scheduling**. The scheduler is an algorithm that uses criteria such as filters to decide where to physically start a task.

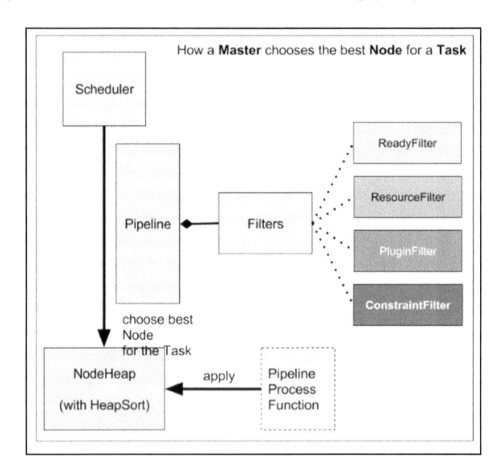

The heart of SwarmKit: swarmd

The core binary to start a SwarmKit service is called `swarmd`, and that's the daemon to create both the master and join slaves.

It can bind itself either to a local UNIX socket and to a TCP socket, but in both cases, is manageable by the `swarmctl` utility by connecting to (another) dedicated UNIX local socket.

In the example that follows in the next section, we'll use swarmd to create a first manager listening on port 4242/tcp, and then again we'll use swarmd on the other worker nodes, to make them join the manager, and finally we'll use swarmctl to check some facts about our cluster.

These binaries are encapsulated into the fsoppelsa/swarmkit image that's available on the Docker Hub, and that we're going to use here to simplify the explanation and avoid Go code compilation.

This is the online help for swarmd. It's rather self-explanatory in its tunables, so we're not going to cover all options in detail. For our practical purposes, the most important options are --listen-remote-api, defining the address:port for swarmd to bind on, and --join-addr, used from other nodes to join the cluster.

```
➜  ~ docker run -ti fsoppelsa/swarmkit swarmd --help
Run a swarm control process

Usage:
  swarmd [flags]

Flags:
  -c, --ca-hash string            Specifies the remote CA root certificate hash, necessary to join the cluster securely
      --election-tick value       Defines the amount of ticks (in seconds) needed without a Leader to trigger a new election (default 3)
      --engine-addr string        Address of engine instance of agent. (default "unix:///var/run/docker.sock")
      --external-ca value         Specifications of one or more certificate signing endpoints
      --force-new-cluster         Force the creation of a new cluster from data directory
      --heartbeat-tick value      Defines the heartbeat interval (in seconds) for raft member health-check (default 1)
      --hostname string           Override reported agent hostname
      --join-addr string          Join cluster with a node at this address
      --listen-control-api string Listen socket for control API (default "./swarmkitstate/swarmd.sock")
      --listen-debug string       Bind the Go debug server on the provided address
      --listen-remote-api string  Listen address for remote API (default "0.0.0.0:4242")
  -l, --log-level string          Log level (options "debug", "info", "warn", "error", "fatal", "panic") (default "info")
      --manager                   Request initial CSR in a manager role
  -s, --secret string             Specifies the secret token required to join the cluster
  -d, --state-dir string          State directory (default "./swarmkitstate")
  -v, --version                   Display the version and exit
➜  ~
```

The controller of SwarmKit: swarmctl

swarmctl is the client part of SwarmKit. It's the tool to use for operating SwarmKit clusters, as it is capable of showing the list of joined nodes, the list of services and tasks, and other information. Here, again from fsoppelsa/swarmkit, the swarmctl online help:

```
→ ~ docker run -ti fsoppelsa/swarmkit swarmctl --help
Control a swarm cluster

Usage:
  swarmctl [command]

Available Commands:
  node       Node management
  service    Service management
  task       Task management
  version    Print version number of swarm
  network    Network management
  cluster    Cluster management

Flags:
  -n, --no-resolve      Do not try to map IDs to Names when displaying them
  -s, --socket string   Socket to connect to the Swarm manager (default "./swarmkitstate/swarmd.sock")

Use "swarmctl [command] --help" for more information about a command.
→ ~
```

Provisioning a SwarmKit cluster with Ansible

In this section, we'll provision a SwarmKit cluster initially made of a single manager and an arbitrary number of slaves.

To create such a setup, we'll use Ansible to make operations repeatable and more robust and, besides illustrating the commands, we'll proceed by examining the playbooks structure. You can easily adapt those playbooks to run on your provider or locally, but here we'll go on Amazon EC2.

To make this example run, there are some basic requirements.

If you want to follow the example on AWS, of course you must have an AWS account and have the access keys configured. Keys are retrievable from the AWS Console under your **Account Name | Security Credentials**. You will need to copy the following key's values:

- Access Key ID
- Secret Access Key

I use `awsctl` to set those keys. Just install it from *brew* (Mac) or from your packaging system if you're using Linux or Windows, and configure it:

```
aws configure
```

Answer the prompt questions by pasting the keys when required. Configuration, where you can specify, for example, a favorite AWS region (such as `us-west-1`) is stored in `~/.aws/config`, while credentials are in `~/.aws/credentials`. In this way, keys are configured and read automatically by Docker Machine.

If you want to run the Ansible example instead of the commands, these are the software requirements:

- Ansible 2.2+
- A Docker client compatible with the image that docker-machine will install on EC2 (in our case, the default one is Ubuntu 15.04 LTS), at the time of writing, the Docker Client 1.11.2
- Docker-machine
- Docker-py client (that's used by Ansible), can be installed with `pip install docker-py`

Moreover, the example is using the standard port `4242/tcp`, to make the cluster nodes interact with each other. So it's required to open that port in a security group.

Clone the repository at `https://github.com/fsoppelsa/ansible-swarmkit` and begin by setting up the SwarmKit Manager node:

```
ansible-playbook aws_provision_master.yml
```

```
$ cd ansible-swarmkit/
$ ansible-playbook aws_provision_master.yml
 [WARNING]: provided hosts list is empty, only localhost is available


PLAY [Provision a Swarmkit master on Amazon EC2] *******************************

TASK [Provision the master host on EC2] ****************************************
changed: [localhost]

TASK [command] *****************************************************************
changed: [localhost]

TASK [set_fact] ****************************************************************
ok: [localhost]

TASK [Run the Swarmkit Master] *************************************************
changed: [localhost]

PLAY RECAP *********************************************************************
localhost                  : ok=4    changed=3    unreachable=0    failed=0

$
```

After some docker-machine setup, the playbook will start a container on the Manager host, acting as a SwarmKit Manager. Here is the play snippet:

```
- name: Run the Swarmkit Master
  docker:
  name: swarmkit-master
  image: "fsoppelsa/swarmkit"
  command: swarmd --listen-remote-api 0.0.0.0:4242
  expose:
    - "4242"
  ports:
    - "0.0.0.0:4242:4242/tcp"
```

```
volumes:
  - "/var/run/docker.sock:/var/run/docker.sock"
detach: yes
docker_url: "{{ dhost }}"
use_tls: encrypt
tls_ca_cert: "{{ dcert }}/ca.pem"
tls_client_cert: "{{ dcert }}/cert.pem"
tls_client_key: "{{ dcert }}/key.pem"
```

On host, a container named `swarmkit-master` from the image `fsoppelsa/swarmkit` runs `swarmd` in manager mode (it listens at `0.0.0.0:4242`). The `swarmd` binary uses the Docker Engine on host directly, so Engine's socket is mounted inside container. The container maps port `4242` to the host port `4242`, so that `swarmd` is reachable by slaves directly by connecting to the host `4242` port.

In practice, it's the equivalent of this Docker command:

```
docker run -d -v /var/run/docker.sock:/var/run/docker.sock -p
4242:4242 fsoppelsa/swarmkit swarmd --listen-remote-api
0.0.0.0:4242
```

This command runs in detached mode (`-d`), passes via volumes (`-v`) the Docker machine Docker socket inside the container, exposes port `4242` from container to host (`-p`), and runs `swarmd` by putting the container itself in listening mode on any address, on port `4242`.

Once the playbook has finished, you can source the `swarmkit-master` machine credentials and check whether our container is running correctly:

```
$ eval $(docker-machine env swarmkit-master)
$ docker ps
CONTAINER ID      IMAGE                 COMMAND               CREATED
    STATUS            PORTS                 NAMES
79d9be555dab      fsoppelsa/swarmkit    "swarmd --listen-remo"  3 minutes ago
    Up 36 seconds     0.0.0.0:4242->4242/tcp   swarmkit-master
$
```

Now it's time to join some slaves. To start a slave, you can, guess what, just run:

```
ansible-playbook aws_provision_slave.yml
```

But since we want to join at least several nodes to the SwarmKit cluster, we go with a little bit of shell scripting:

```
for i in $(seq 5); do ansible-playbook aws_provision_slave.yml;
done
```

This command runs five times the playbook, thus creating five worker nodes. The playbook, after creating a machine named swarmkit-RANDOM will start a fsoppelsa/swarmkit container doing the following:

```
- name: Join the slave to the Swarmkit cluster
  docker:
    name: "{{machine_uuid}}"
    image: "fsoppelsa/swarmkit"
    command: swarmd --join-addr "{{ masterip }}":4242
    volumes:
      - "/var/run/docker.sock:/var/run/docker.sock"
    detach: yes
    docker_url: "{{ shost }}"
```

Here, swarmd runs in join mode, and joins the cluster initiated on the Master, by connecting to port 4242/tcp. This is the equivalent of the following docker command:

```
docker run -d -v /var/run/docker.sock:/var/run/docker.sock
fsoppelsa/swarmkit swarmd --join-addr $(docker-machine ip swarmkit-
master):4242
```

The ansible loop command will take some minutes to finish, depending on how many workers are starting. When the playbook has finished, we can control that the cluster was created correctly using swarmctl. If you haven't sourced the swarmkit-master Machine credential yet, it's time to:

```
eval $(docker-machine env swarmkit-master)
```

Now we invoke the container running the swarmd master, using exec:

```
docker exec -ti 79d9be555dab swarmctl -s /swarmkitstate/swarmd.sock
node ls
```

```
●●●                          1. root@anakin:~ (ssh)
$ docker ps
CONTAINER ID        IMAGE               COMMAND               CREATED        STATUS
          PORTS                  NAMES
79d9be555dab        fsoppelsa/swarmkit  "swarmd --listen-remo"  2 days ago     Up 2 days
          0.0.0.0:4242->4242/tcp    swarmkit-master
$ docker exec -ti 79d9be555dab swarmctl -s /swarmkitstate/swarmd.sock node ls
ID                         Name                   Membership  Status  Availability  Manager Status
--                         ----                   ----------  ------  ------------  --------------
3fm2amywezv6sy8p88blmssul  swarmkit-9f13f6d3      ACCEPTED    READY   ACTIVE
4qj8u9wtd2akkfoukv1bv66kq  swarmkit-ae4a3c86      ACCEPTED    READY   ACTIVE
549xqbs5trxtutk5204ifetj3  swarmkit-ba7d547e      ACCEPTED    READY   ACTIVE
7s1a8gcrm5wuerxl2egbp51ta  swarmkit-b4802b2f      ACCEPTED    READY   ACTIVE
bkab9maxaj1patti8nv0wibl3  swarmkit-1ad04abd      ACCEPTED    READY   ACTIVE
e9xscs6e7u4hrkdugepjaeroc  swarmkit-master        ACCEPTED    READY   ACTIVE        REACHABLE *
er1t2hm4vtq8pj1jhjv6vv71c  swarmkit-3ba2db01      ACCEPTED    READY   ACTIVE
$ ▊
```

So, here we have listed the workers that have joined the master.

Creating a service on SwarmKit

Using the usual `swarmctl` binary, we can now create a service (web), made of nginx containers.

We begin by checking to make sure that there are no active services on this brand new cluster:

```
●●●                          1. root@anakin:~ (ssh)
$ docker exec -ti 79d9be555dab swarmctl service ls
ID  Name  Image  Replicas
--  ----  -----  --------
$ ▊
```

So we're ready to start one, with this command:

```
docker exec -ti 79d9be555dab swarmctl service create --name web --
image nginx --replicas 5
```

```
● ● ●                          1. root@anakin:~ (ssh)
$ docker exec -ti 79d9be555dab swarmctl service create --name web --image nginx --replicas 5
2ylsymmljv3t6bux43d7aqkba
$
```

This command specifies to create a service named web, made of nginx container images, and replicate it with a factor of 5, so as to create 5 nginx containers across the cluster. It will take some seconds to take effect, because on each node of the cluster, Swarm will pull and start the nginx image, but finally:

```
● ● ●                    1. root@anakin:~ (ssh)
$ docker exec -ti 79d9be555dab swarmctl service ls
ID                           Name   Image   Replicas

--                           ----   -----   --------
2ylsymmljv3t6bux43d7aqkba    web    nginx   5/5
$
```

The **5/5** indicates that of 5 desired replicas, 5 are up. We can see in detail where those containers got spawned using swarmctl task ls:

```
● ● ●                          1. root@anakin:~ (ssh)
$ docker exec -ti 79d9be555dab swarmctl task ls
ID                          Service  Desired State  Last State            Node
--                          -------  -------------  ----------            ----
1a8itqd2nni4wwlig8pntfouw   web.5    RUNNING        RUNNING 5 minutes ago  swarmkit-master
5tt5yu3250ym492e481899180   web.4    RUNNING        RUNNING 5 minutes ago  swarmkit-ae4a3c86
btf5lzk6w347wygbb82ch6su3   web.2    RUNNING        RUNNING 5 minutes ago  swarmkit-3ba2db01
cc267di5cz9ugjckn3ywacbvd   web.3    RUNNING        RUNNING 5 minutes ago  swarmkit-b4802b2f
e62tfxrb5b5fjy5axgxe23391   web.1    RUNNING        RUNNING 5 minutes ago  swarmkit-9f13f6d3
$
```

But, wait, is a nginx service (web.5) running on the manager node? Yes. SwarmKit and Swarm Mode managers are allowed to run tasks, by default, and the scheduler can dispatch jobs onto them.

In a real production configuration, if you want to reserve managers to not run jobs, you need to apply a configuration with labels and constraints. This is a topic of `Chapter 5`, *Administer a Swarm Cluster*.

Swarm mode

Docker Swarm mode (for Docker Engines of version 1.12 or newer) imports the SwarmKit libraries in order to make distributed container orchestration over multiple hosts possible and easy to operate.

The main difference between SwarmKit and Swarm Mode is that Swarm Mode is integrated into Docker itself, starting from version 1.12. This means that Swarm Mode commands such as `swarm`, `nodes`, `service`, and `task` are available *inside* the Docker client, and that through the docker command it's possible to initiate and manage Swarms, as well as deploy services and tasks:

- `docker swarm init`: This is to initialize a Swarm cluster
- `docker node ls`: This is used to list the available nodes
- `docker service tasks`: This is used to list the tasks associated to a specific service

Old versus new Swarm versus SwarmKit

At the time of writing, (August 2016), we have three Docker orchestration systems: the old one (that is) Swarm v1, SwarmKit, and the new one (that is) integrated Swarm Mode.

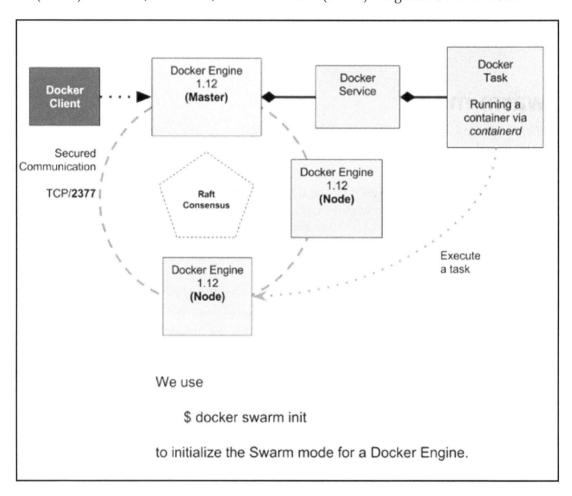

The original Swarm v1, the one we showed in Chapter 1, *Welcome to Docker Swarm* and that's still used around, is not yet deprecated. It's a way of using (recycling?) older infrastructures. But starting from Docker 1.12, the new Swarm Mode is the recommended way to begin a new orchestration project, especially if it will need to scale to a big size.

To make things simpler, let's summarize the differences between these projects with some tables.

First, the old Swarm v1 versus the new Swarm Mode:

Swarm standalone	Swarm Mode
This is available since Docker 1.8	This is available since Docker 1.12
This is available as a container	This is integrated into the Docker Engine
This needs an external discovery service (such as Consul, Etcd, or Zookeeper)	This doesn't need an external discovery service, Etcd integrated
This is not secure by default	This is secure by default
The replica and scaling features are not available	The replica and scaling features are available
There are no service and task concepts for modeling microservices	There are out of the box services, tasks, load balancing, and service discovery
There is no additional networking available	This has integrated VxLAN (mesh networking)

And now, to clarify ideas, let's compare SwarmKit and Swarm mode:

SwarmKit	Swarm mode
These are released as binaries (`swarmd` and `swarmctl`)–use swarmctl	These are integrated into the Docker Engine–use docker
These are generic tasks	These are container tasks
These include services and tasks	These include services and tasks
These include no service advanced features, such as load balancing and VxLAN networking	These include out of the box service advanced features, such as load balancing and VxLAN networking

Swarm Mode zoom in

As we already summarized in the preceding table in Swarm standalone versus Swarm mode comparison, the main new features available in Swarm Mode are the integration into the engine, no need for an external discovery service, and replica, scale, load balancing, and networking included.

Integration into the engine

With docker 1.12+, some new commands are added to the docker client. We now take a survey on the ones that are relevant to the matter of this book.

docker swarm command

This is the current command to manage Swarms:

```
➡ ~ docker swarm --help

Usage:  docker swarm COMMAND

Manage Docker Swarm

Options:
      --help    Print usage

Commands:
  init          Initialize a swarm
  join          Join a swarm as a node and/or manager
  join-token    Manage join tokens
  update        Update the swarm
  leave         Leave a swarm

Run 'docker swarm COMMAND --help' for more information on a command.
```

It accepts the following options:

- `init`: This initializes a Swarm. Behind the curtain, this command creates a manager for the current Docker host and generates a *secret* (its password that workers will pass to the API so as to be authorized to join the cluster).
- `join`: This is used by a worker to join a cluster, must specify the *secret* and a list of managers IP port values.
- `join-token`: This is used to manage the `join-tokens`. `join-tokens` are special token secrets used to make join managers or workers (managers and workers have different token values). This command is a convenient way to make Swarm print the necessary command to join a manager or a worker:

```
docker swarm join-token worker
```

To add a worker to this swarm, run the following command:

```
docker swarm join \ --token SWMTKN-1-
36gj6glgi3ub2i28ekm1b1er8aa51vltv00760t7umh3wmo1sc-
aucj6a94tqhhn2k0iipnc6096 \ 192.168.65.2:2377
docker swarm join-token manager
```

To add a manager to this swarm, run the following command:

```
docker swarm join \ --token SWMTKN-1-
36gj6glgi3ub2i28ekm1b1er8aa51vltv00760t7umh3wmo1sc-
98glton0ot50j1yn8eci48rvq \ 192.168.65.2:2377
```

- `update`: This updates the cluster by changing some of its values, for example, you can use it to specify a new URL of the certificate endpoint
- `leave`: This commands the current node to leave the cluster. If something is blocking the operation, there is a useful `--force` option.

docker node

This is the command to handle swarm nodes. You must launch it from a manager, so you need to be connected to a manager in order to use it.

```
➜ ~ docker node --help

Usage:  docker node COMMAND

Manage Docker Swarm nodes

Options:
      --help    Print usage

Commands:
  demote      Demote a node from manager in the swarm
  inspect     Display detailed information on one or more nodes
  ls          List nodes in the swarm
  promote     Promote a node to a manager in the swarm
  rm          Remove a node from the swarm
  ps          List tasks running on a node
  update      Update a node

Run 'docker node COMMAND --help' for more information on a command.
```

- `demote` and `promote`: These are commands used to manage the status of nodes. With that mechanism, you can promote a node to a manager, or demote it to a worker. In practice, Swarm will try to `demote/promote`. We will cover this concept just a bit later in this chapter.
- `inspect`: This is the equivalent of docker info, but for a Swarm node. It prints information regarding the node/s.
- `ls`: This lists the nodes connected to the cluster.
- `rm`: This attempts to remove a worker. If you want to remove a manager, you have before to demote it to worker.
- `ps`: This shows the list of tasks running on a specified node.
- `update`: This allows you to change some configuration values for a node, namely tags.

docker service

This is the command to manage the services running on a Swarm cluster:

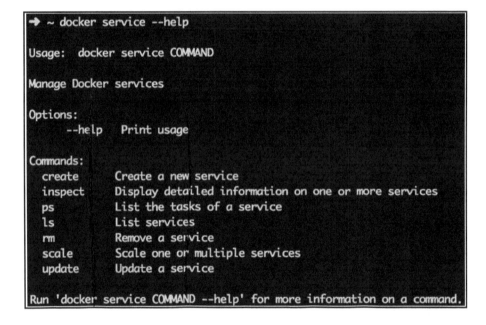

```
➜  ~ docker service --help

Usage:  docker service COMMAND

Manage Docker services

Options:
      --help    Print usage

Commands:
  create      Create a new service
  inspect     Display detailed information on one or more services
  ps          List the tasks of a service
  ls          List services
  rm          Remove a service
  scale       Scale one or multiple services
  update      Update a service

Run 'docker service COMMAND --help' for more information on a command.
```

Apart from the expected commands such as `create`, `inspect`, `ps`, `ls`, `rm`, and `update`, there is a new interesting one: `scale`.

Docker Stack

Not directly necessary to Swarm operations, but introduced as experimental in Docker 1.12, there is the `stack` command. Stacks are now bundles of containers. For example, a nginx + php + mysql container setup can be stacked in a self-contained Docker Stack, called **Distributed Application Bundle** (**DAB**) and described by a JSON file.

The core command of docker stack will be deploy, thanks to which it will be possible to create and update DABs. We'll meet stacks later in `Chapter 6`, *Deploy Real Applications on Swarm*.

Etcd's Raft is integrated already

Docker Swarm Mode already integrates RAFT through CoreOS Etcd Raft library. There is no further need to integrate external discovery services such as Zookeeper or Consul anymore. Swarm directly takes care of essential services such as DNS and load balancing.

Installing a Swarm Mode cluster is just a matter of starting Docker hosts and running Docker commands, making it super easy to set up.

Load balancing and DNS

By design, the cluster managers assign to every service in the swarm a unique DNS name and load balances running containers, using an internal DNS to Docker. Queries and resolutions work automatically out of the box.

For each service created with a `--name myservice`, every container in the swarm will be able to resolve the service IP address just as they were resolving (`dig myservice`) internal network names, using the Docker embedded DNS server. So, if you have a `nginx-service` (made of nginx containers, for example), you can just `ping nginx-service` to reach the frontend head.

Also, in Swarm mode, operators have the possibility to `publish` services ports to an external load balancer. Ports are then exposed outside to a port in a range from `30000` to `32767`. Internally, Swarm uses iptables and IPVS to execute packet filtering and forwarding, and load balancing respectively.

Iptables is the default packet filter firewall used by Linux while IPVS is the seasoned IP Virtual Server defined in the Linux kernel, that can be used for load balancing traffic, and that's just what Docker Swarm uses.

Ports are published either when a new service is created or updated, using the `--publish-add` option. With this option, an internal service is published, and gets load balanced.

For example, if we have a cluster with three workers each running nginx (on a service named `nginx-service`), we can expose their target-port to the load balancer with:

```
docker service update --port-add 80 nginx-service
```

This will create a mapping between the published port `30000` on any of the nodes cluster, and the `nginx` containers (port 80). If you connect any node to port `30000`, you will be greeted by the Nginx welcome page.

But how does this work? As you see in the preceding screenshot, there is an associated VirtualIP (`10.255.0.7/16`), or VIP, and it is collocated on the overlay network **2xbr2upsr3yl**, created by Swarm for ingress to the load balancer:

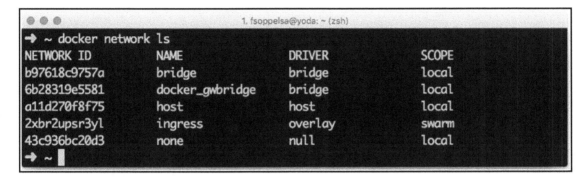

From any host, you are able to reach `nginx-service`, because the DNS name resolves to the VIP, here 10.255.0.7, acting as a frontend to the load balancer:

On each node of the swarm, Swarm implements load balancing in kernel, specifically inside the namespaces, by adding a MARK rule in the OUTPUT chain inside the network namespace dedicated to the network, as shown in the following screenshot:

We'll cover networking concepts in greater detail later, in `Chapter 5`, *Administer a Swarm Cluster* and `Chapter 8`, *Exploring Additional features of Swarm*.

Promotion and demotion

With the `docker node` command, the cluster operator can promote nodes from workers to managers and, vice versa, demote them from managers to workers.

Demoting a node from manager to worker is the only way to remove a manager (now worker) from the cluster.

We'll cover promotion and demotion operations in detail in `Chapter 5`, *Administer a Swarm Cluster*.

Replicas and scale

Deploying an app on a Swarm cluster means to define and configure services, start them and wait for Docker engines scattered across the cluster to launch containers. We'll deploy complete apps on Swarm in Chapter 6, *Deploy Real Applications on Swarm*.

Services and tasks

The core of the Swarm workload is divided into services. A service is just an abstraction to group an arbitrary number of tasks (this number is called the *replica factor*, or just *replicas*). Tasks are running containers.

docker service scale

With the docker service scale command, you order Swarm to ensure that a certain number of replicas are running at the same time on the cluster. For example, you can start with 10 containers running some *task* distributed over the cluster, and then when you need to scale their size to 30 you just execute:

```
docker service scale myservice=30
```

Swarm is ordered to schedule 20 new containers, so it takes the appropriate decisions for load balancing, DNS, and networking coherence. If a container for *task* goes down, making the replica factor equal to 29, Swarm will reschedule another one on another cluster node (that will have a new ID) to maintain the factor equal to 30.

A note on replicas and new nodes addition. People frequently ask about Swarm automatic capabilities. If you have five workers running 30 tasks, and add five new nodes, you should not expect Swarm to balance the 30 tasks across the new nodes automatically, moving them from the original to the new nodes. The behavior of the Swarm scheduler is conservative, until some event (for example, an operator intervention) triggers a new scale command. Only in that case, the scheduler will take into account the five new nodes and possibly start new replica tasks on the 5 new workers.

We'll see how scale command works in practice in Chapter 7, *Scaling Up Your Platform*.

Summary

In this chapter, we met the new actors in the Docker ecosystem: SwarmKit and Swarm Mode. We proceeded through a simple implementation of a SwarmKit cluster with Ansible on Amazon AWS. Then, we covered the essential concepts of Swarm Mode, introducing its interface and its internals, including DNS, load balancing, services, replicas, and the promotion/demotion mechanism. Now, it's time to dive into a true Swarm Mode deployment, as we'll see in `Chapter 4`, *Creating a Production-Grade Swarm*.

4
Creating a Production-Grade Swarm

In this chapter, you will learn how to create real Swarm clusters with thousands of nodes; specifically we'll cover the following topics:

- Tools to deploy large Swarms
- Swarm2k: One of the largest Swarm mode cluster ever built, made of 2,300 nodes
- Swarm3k: The second experiment, a cluster with 4,700 nodes
- How to plan hardware resources
- HA cluster topologies
- Swarm infrastructures management, networking, and security
- Monitoring dashboards
- What you learned from the Swarm2k and Swarm3k experiments

Tools

With Swarm Mode, we can easily design a production-grade cluster.

The principles and architecture we're illustrating here are important in general and give a foundation on how to architect production installations, regardless of the tools. However, from a practical point of view, the tools to use are also important.

At the time of writing this book, Docker Machine was not the ideal single tool to use for large swarms setups, so we're demonstrating our production-scale deployments with a tool born alongside with this book that we already introduced in Chapter 1, *Welcome to Docker Swarm*: belt (https://github.com/chanwit/belt). We'll use it in conjunction with Docker Machine, Docker Networking, and the DigitalOcean's doctl command.

In Chapter 5, *Administer a Swarm Cluster* you'll learn how it's possible to automate the creation of Swarms; especially, how to quickly join a massive number of workers with scripts and other mechanisms, such as Ansible.

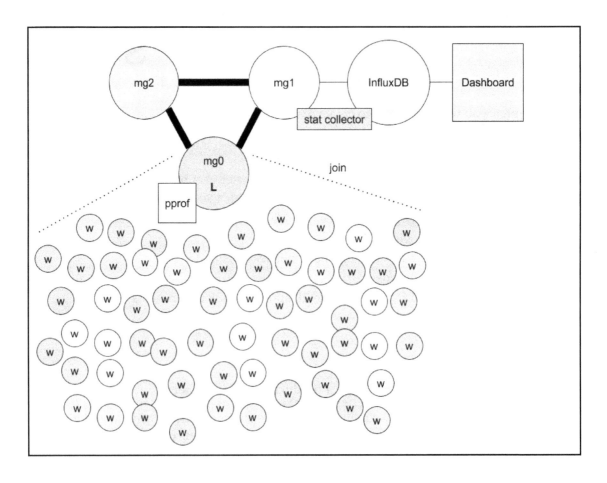

An HA Topology for Swarm2k

Swarm2k and Swarm3k were collaborative experiments. We raised funds in terms of Docker Hosts, instead of money, with a call to participate. The result was astonishing-Swarm2k and Swarm3k were joined by dozens of individuals and corporate geographically distributed contributors. In total, for Swarm2k, we collected around 2,300 nodes, while for Swarm3k, around 4,700.

Let's discuss the architecture of *Swarm2k*. In the preceding figure, there are three managers, denoted as **mg0**, **mg1**, and **mg2**. We will use the three managers because it is the optimum number of managers, suggested by the Docker core team. Managers formed a quorum on a high-speed network link and raft nodes employ employed a significant amount of resources to synchronize their activities. So, we decided to deploy our managers on a 40GB Ethernet link into the same data center.

At the beginning of the experiment, we had the following configuration:

- mg0 was the cluster's manager leader
- mg1 hosted the stat collector
- mg2 was a ready (reserve) manager

Instead, the **W** nodes were Swarm workers.

The stat collector installed on mg1 queries the information out of the local Docker Engine and sends them to store in a remote time-series database, *InfluxDB*. We chose InfluxDB because it's natively supported by *Telegraf*, our monitoring agent. To display the cluster's statistics, we used *Grafana* as a dashboard, which we'll see later.

Managers specifications

Managers are CPU bound rather than memory bound. For a 500-1,000 nodes Swarm cluster, we observed empirically that three managers with 8 vCPUs each are enough to keep the load. However, if it's beyond 2,000 nodes, we recommend, for each manager, at least 16-20 vCPUs to meet eventual Raft recoveries.

In case of Raft recovery

The following diagram shows the CPU usage during a hardware upgrade and under a massive number of workers join process. During the hardware upgrade to 8 vCPUs (the machines downtime is represented by lines disconnections), we can see that the CPU usage of mg0, the leader, spiked to 75-90% when **mg1** and **mg2** rejoined the cluster. The event that triggered this spike is the Raft log synchronization and recovery.

Under normal conditions, with no required recoveries, CPU usage of each manager stays low, as shown in the following image.

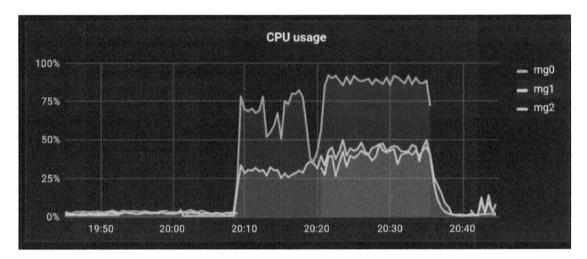

Raft files

In manager hosts, Swarm data is saved in `/var/lib/docker/swarm`, called the *swarm directory*. Specifically, Raft data is saved in `/var/lib/docker/swarm/raft` and consists of the Write Ahead Log (WAL) and snapshot files.

In these files, there are entries for nodes, services, and tasks, as defined by the Protobuf format.

WAL and snapshot files are frequently written to disk. In SwarmKit and Docker Swarm Mode, they are written to disk every 10,000 entries. Per this behavior, we mapped the swarm directory to a fast and dedicated disk with increased throughput, specifically an SSD drive.

We will explain backup and restore procedures in case of the swarm directory corruption in Chapter 5, *Administer a Swarm Cluster*.

Running tasks

The goal of Swarm clusters is to run services, for example, large-scale Web applications made from a big number of containers. We will call this deployment type the *Mono* model. In this model, network ports are considered resources that must be published globally. With *namespaces* in the future versions of Docker Swarm Mode, the deployment can be in the *Multi* model, where we are allowed to have multiple subclusters, which expose the same port for different services.

In small-size clusters, we can decide to allow managers to host worker tasks with some prudence. For larger setups, instead, managers use more resources. Moreover, in case a manager load saturates its resources, the cluster will become unstable and unresponsive and will not take any commands. We call this state the *Berserkstate*.

To make a large cluster, such as Swarm2k or Swarm3k stable, all managers' availability must be set to the "Drained" state so that all the tasks will not be scheduled on them, only on workers, with:

```
docker node update --availability drain node-name
```

Manager topologies

We'll discuss this HA property in `Chapter 5`, *Administer a Swarm Cluster* again, but here, we will introduce it to illustrate some Swarm topologies theory. The HA theory makes it mandatory to form a HA cluster with an odd number of nodes. The following table shows the fault tolerance factors for a single data center. In this chapter, we'll call the 5(1)-3-2 formula for a cluster size of 5 over 1 data center with 3-node quorum that allows 2 nodes to fail:

Cluster Size	Quorum	Node Failure allowed
3	2	1
5	3	2
7	4	3
9	5	4

However, there are several manager topologies that can be designed to use in production environments with multiple data centers. For example, the 3(3) manager topology can be distributed as 1 + 1 + 1, while the 5(3) manager topology can be distributed as 2 + 2 + 1. The following image shows the optimum 5(3) manager topology:

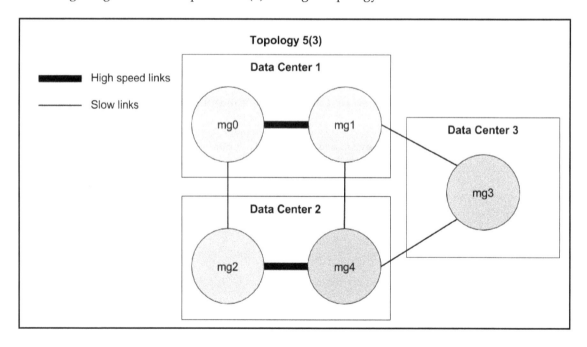

With the same level of tolerance, the next image shows an alternative 5(4) topology containing 5 managers across 4 data centers. There are 2 managers, mg0, and mg1, running in Data Center 1, while each of the remaining managers, mg2, mg3, and mg4, run in Data Center 2, 3, and 4 respectively. The mg0 and mg1 managers are connected on high-speed network, while mg2, mg3, and mg4 can use a slower link. Therefore, 2 + 2 + 1 across 3 data centers will be rearranged as 2 + 1 + 1 + 1 over 4 data centers.

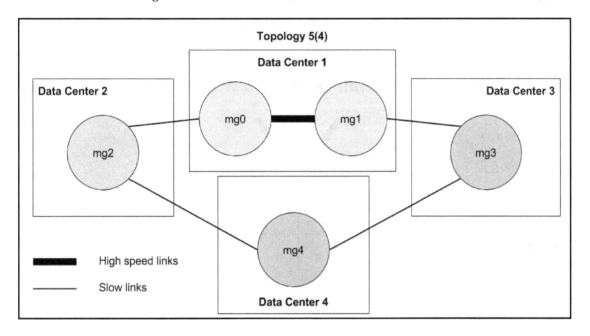

Finally, there is another distributed topology, 6(4), which is much more performant because, at its heart, there are 3 nodes forming a central quorum on high-speed links. The 6-manager cluster needs a quorum size of 4. If Data Center 1 fails, the control plane of the cluster will stop working. In normal case, 2 nodes or 2 data centers, except the main one, can be down.

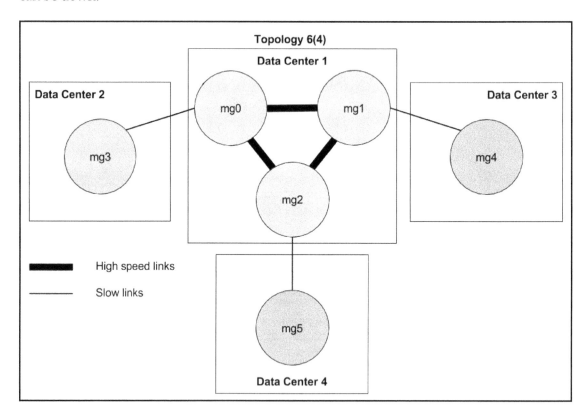

To sum it up, stick with odd numbers of managers whenever possible. If you want stability of manager quorum, form it over high-speed links. If you want to avoid single point of failures, distribute them as much as possible.

To confirm which topology will work for you, try forming it and test the manager latency by intentionally putting some managers down and then measure how fast they recover.

For Swarm2k and Swarm3k, we chose to form topology with all three managers being on a single data center because we wanted to achieve the best performances.

Provisioning the infrastructure with belt

First, we created a cluster template named `swarm2k` for DigitalOcean with the following command:

```
$ belt cluster new --driver digitalocean swarm2k
```

The preceding command creates a configuration template file in the current directory called `.belt/swarm2k/config.yml`. This was our starting point to define other attributes.

We checked if our cluster was defined by running the following command:

```
$ belt cluster ls
CLUSTER        ACTIVE      LEADER      MASTERS     #NODES
swarm2k        -           -           -           0 / 0
```

With the use command, we can switch and used the available `swarm2k` clusters, as follows:

```
$ belt use swarm2k
swarm2k
```

At this point, we refined the `swarm2k` template's attributes.

By setting the DigitalOcean's instance region to be `sgp1` by issuing the following command:

```
$ belt cluster update region=sgp1
```

Belt required to define all necessary values with this command. Here's a list of the required template keys for the DigitalOcean driver that we specified in `config.yml`:

- `image`: This is to specify the DigitalOcean image ID or snapshot ID
- `region`: This is to specify the DigitalOcean region, for example, sgp1 or nyc3
- `ssh_key_fingerprint`: This is to specify the DigitalOcean SSH Key ID or fingerprint
- `ssh_user`: This is to specify the username used by the image, for example, root
- `access_token`: This is to specify DigitalOcean's access token; it is recommended to not put any of the tokens here

Every template attribute has its environment variable counterpart. For example, the `access_token` attribute can be set via `DIGITALOCEAN_ACCESS_TOKEN`. So, in practice, we can also export `DIGITALOCEAN_ACCESS_TOKEN` as a shell variable before proceeding.

With the configuration in place, we verified the current template attributes by running the following piece of code:

```
$ belt cluster config
digitalocean:
  image: "123456"
  region: sgp1
  ssh_key_fingerprint: "800000"
  ssh_user: root
```

Now, we created a set of 3 512MB manger nodes called mg0, mg1, and mg2 with the following syntax:

```
$ belt create 8192MB mg[0:2]
NAME   IPv4          MEMORY  REGION  IMAGE             STATUS
mg2    128.*.*.11    8192    sgp1    Ubuntu docker-1.12.1 new
mg1    128.*.*.220   8192    sgp1    Ubuntu docker-1.12.1 new
mg0    128.*.*.21    8192    sgp1    Ubuntu docker-1.12.1 new
```

All new nodes are initialized and go to a new status.

We can use the following command to wait until all 3 nodes become active:

```
$ belt status --wait active=3
STATUS   #NODES   NAMES
new          3    mg2, mg1, mg0
STATUS   #NODES   NAMES
new          3    mg2, mg1, mg0
STATUS   #NODES   NAMES
new          3    mg2, mg1, mg0
STATUS   #NODES   NAMES
active       3    mg2, mg1, mg0
```

Then, we set node1 to be the active manger host, and our Swarm will be ready to be formed. Setting the active host can be done by running the active command, as follows:

```
$ belt active mg0
swarm2k/mg0
```

At this point, we formed a swarm. We initialized mg0 as the manager leader, as follows:

```
$ belt docker swarm init --advertise-addr 128.*.*.220
Swarm initialized: current node (24j7sytbomhshtayt74lf7njo) is now
a manager.
```

The preceding command outputs the strings to copy and paste to join other managers and workers, for example, take a look at the following command:

```
docker swarm join \
--token SWMTKN-1-1wwyxnfcgqt...fwzc1in3 \
128.*.*.220:2377
```

Belt provides a convenient shortcut to join nodes with the following syntax, that was what we used to join mg1 and mg2 to the swarm.:

```
$ belt --host mg[1:2] docker swarm join \
--token --token SWMTKN-1-1wwyxnfcgqt...fwzc1in3 \
128.*.*.220:2377
```

Now, we have the mg0, mg1, and mg2 managers configured and ready to get the swarm of workers.

Securing Managers with Docker Machine

Docker Machine won't scale well for massive Docker Engine deployments, but it turns out to be very useful for automatically securing small number of nodes. In the following section, we'll use Docker Machine to secure our Swarm manager using the generic driver, a driver that allows us to control existing hosts.

In our case, we already did set up a Docker Swarm manager on mg0. Furthermore, we want to secure Docker Engine by enabling the TLS connection for its remote endpoint.

How can Docker Machine do the work for us? First, Docker Machine connects to the host via SSH; detects the operating system of mg0, in our case, Ubuntu; and the provisioner, in our case, systemd.

After that, it installs the Docker Engine; however, in case one is already in place, like here, it will skip this step.

Then, as the most important part, it generates a Root CA certificate, as well as all certificates, and stores them on the host. It also automatically configures Docker to use those certificates. Finally, it restarts Docker.

If everything goes well, Docker Engine will be started again with TLS enabled.

We then used Docker Machine to generate a Root CA for the Engine on mg0, mg1 and mg2, and configure a TLS connection. Then, we later used the Docker client to further control Swarm without the need of SSH, which is slower.

```
$ docker-machine create \
  --driver generic \
  --generic-ip-address=$(belt ip mg0) mg0
Running pre-create checks...
Creating machine...
(mg0) No SSH key specified. Assuming an existing key at the default
location.
Waiting for machine to be running, this may take a few minutes...
Detecting operating system of created instance...
Waiting for SSH to be available...
Detecting the provisioner...
Provisioning with ubuntu(systemd)...
Installing Docker...
Copying certs to the local machine directory...
Copying certs to the remote machine...
Setting Docker configuration on the remote daemon...
Checking connection to Docker...
Then we can test our working swarm with `docker info`. We grep only
15 lines for the brevity.
$ docker $(docker-machine config mg0) info | grep -A 15 Swarm
Swarm: active
 NodeID: 24j7sytbomhshtayt741f7njo
 Is Manager: true
 ClusterID: 8rshkwfq4hsil2tdb3idpqdeg
 Managers: 3
 Nodes: 3
 Orchestration:
  Task History Retention Limit: 5
 Raft:
  Snapshot Interval: 10000
  Heartbeat Tick: 1
  Election Tick: 3
 Dispatcher:
  Heartbeat Period: 5 seconds
 CA Configuration:
  Expiry Duration: 3 months
```

Also, `docker node ls` will work normally with this setup We verified now that the 3 managers formed the initial swarm, and were able to accept a bunch of workers:

```
$ docker $(docker-machine config mg0) node ls
ID                          HOSTNAME  STATUS  AVAILABILITY  MANAGER STATUS
24j7sytbomhshtayt741f7njo * mg0       Ready   Active        Leader
2a4jcvp32aoa6olaxlelthkws   mg1       Ready   Active        Reachable
94po1ln0j0g5fgjnjfvm1w02r   mg2       Ready   Active        Reachable
```

How secure is this cluster?

We will use the Docker client to connect to the Docker Engine equipped TLS; and, there's another TLS connection among the swarm's node with CA expiring in three months, and it will be auto-rotated. Advanced security setup will be discussed in `Chapter 9`, *Securing a Swarm Cluster and the Docker Software Supply Chain*.

Understanding some Swarm internals

At this point, we checked that the Swarm was operative, by creating a service nginx with 3 replicas:

```
$ eval $(docker-machine env mg0)
$ docker service create --name nginx --replicas 3 nginx
du2luca34cmy
```

Afteer that, we found where the net namespace ID of the running Nginx was. We connected to mg0 via SSH to mg0 via SSH. The network namespace for Swarm's routing mesh was the one having the same timestamp as the special network namespace, `1-5t4znibozx`. In this example, the namespace we're looking for is `fe3714ca42d0`.

```
root@mg0:~# ls /var/run/docker/netns -al
total 0
drwxr-xr-x 2 root root 120 Aug 22 15:38 .
drwx------ 5 root root 100 Aug 22 13:39 ..
-r--r--r-- 1 root root   0 Aug 22 15:17 1-5t4znibozx
-r--r--r-- 1 root root   0 Aug 22 15:36 d9ef48834a31
-r--r--r-- 1 root root   0 Aug 22 15:17 fe3714ca42d0
```

We can figure out our IPVS entries with ipvsadm, and run it inside the net namespace using the nsenter tool (`https://github.com/jpetazzo/nsenter`), as follows:

```
root@node1:~# nsenter --net=/var/run/docker/netns/fe3714ca42d0 ipvsadm
-L
IP Virtual Server version 1.2.1 (size=4096)
Prot LocalAddress:Port Scheduler Flags
  -> RemoteAddress:Port             Forward Weight ActiveConn InActConn
FWM  259 rr
  -> 10.255.0.8:0                   Masq    1       0           2
```

Here, we can notice that there is an active round-robin IPVS entry. IPVS is the kernel-level load balancer, and it's used by Swarm to balance traffic in conjunction with iptables, which is used to forward and filter packets.

After cleaning the nginx test service (`docker service rm nginx`), we will set the managers in Drain mode, so to avoid them to take tasks:

```
$ docker node update --availability drain mg0
$ docker node update --availability drain mg1
$ docker node update --availability drain mg2
```

Now, we are ready to announce the availability of our managers on Twitter and Github and start the experiment!

Joining workers

Our contributors started joining their nodes to manager **mg0** as workers. Anyone used their own favorite method, including the following:

- Looping `docker-machine ssh sudo docker swarm join` commands
- Ansible
- Custom scripts and programs

We'll cover some of these methods in `Chapter 5`, *Administer a Swarm Cluster* .

After some time, we reached the quota of 2,300 workers and launched an **alpine** service with a replica factor of 100,000:

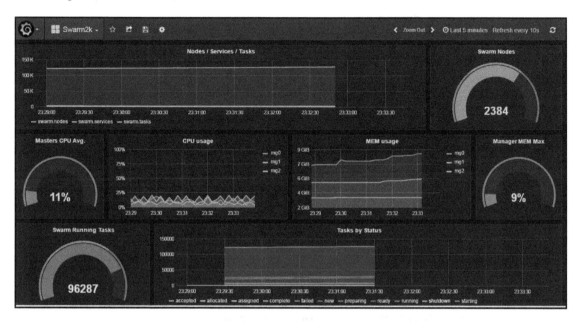

Upgrading Managers

After some time, we reached the maximum of capacity for our managers, and we had to increase their physical resources. Live upgrading and maintenance of managers may be an expected operation in production. Here is how we did this operation.

Live Upgrading the Managers

With an odd number for the quorum, it is safe to demote a manager for maintenance.

```
$ docker node ls
ID                      HOSTNAME  STATUS  AVAILABILITY  MANAGER STATUS
4viybni..h24zxde        mg1       Ready   Active        Reachable
6xxwumb..j6zvtyg *      mg0       Ready   Active        Leader
f1vs2e3..abdehnh        mg2       Ready   Active
```

Here, we had mg1 as a reachable manager, and we demoted it to worker with the following syntax:

```
$ docker node demote mg1
Manager mg1 demoted in the swarm.
```

We can see that the `Reachable` status of `mg1` disappears from node ls output when it becomes a worker.

```
$ docker node ls
ID                    HOSTNAME    STATUS  AVAILABILITY  MANAGER STATUS
4viybni..h24zxde      mg1         Ready   Active
6xxwumb..j6zvtyg *    mg0         Ready   Active        Leader
f1vs2e3..abdehnh      mg2         Ready   Active
```

When the node is not a manager anymore, it's safe to shut it down, for example, with the DigitalOcean CLI, as we did:

```
$ doctl compute droplet-action shutdown 23362382
```

Listing the nodes, we noticed that mg1 was already down.

```
$ docker node ls
ID                            HOSTNAME  STATUS  AVAILABILITY  MANAGER STATUS
4viybni0ud2gjpay6ih24zxde     mg1       Down    Active
6xxwumbdac34bbgh6hj6zvtyg *   mg0       Ready   Active        Leader
f1vs2e3hjiqjaukmjqabdehnh     mg2       Ready   Active
```

We upgraded its resources to have 16G of memory, and then we powered the machine on again:

```
$ doctl -c .doctlcfg compute droplet-action power-on 23362382
```

When listing this time, we can expect some delay as mg1 is being back and reentered the cluster.

```
$ docker node ls
ID                    HOSTNAME    STATUS  AVAILABILITY  MANAGER STATUS
4viybni..h24zxde      mg1         Ready   Active
6xxwumb..j6zvtyg *    mg0         Ready   Active        Leader
f1vs2e3..abdehnh      mg2         Ready   Active
```

Finally, we can promote it back to the manager, as follows:

```
$ docker node promote mg1
Node mg1 promoted to a manager in the swarm.
```

Once this is done, the cluster operated normally. So, we repeated the operation for mg0 and mg2.

Monitoring Swarm2k

For the production-grade cluster, we usually want to set up some kind of monitoring. At the date, there is not a specific way to monitor Docker service and tasks in Swarm mode. We did this for Swarm2k with Telegraf, InfluxDB, and Grafana.

InfluxDB Time-Series Database

InfluxDB is a time-series database, which is easy to install because of no dependency. InfluxDB is useful to store metrics, information about events, and use them for later analysis. For Swarm2k, we used InfluxDB to store information of cluster, nodes, events, and for tasks with Telegraf.

Telegraf is pluggable and has a certain number of input plugins useful to observe the system environment.

Telegraf Swarm plugin

We developed a new plugin for Telegraf to store stats into InfluxDB. This plugin can be found at `http://github.com/chanwit/telegraf`. Data may contain *values*, *tags*, and *timestamp*. Values will be computed or aggregated based on timestamp. Additionally, tags will allow you to group these values together based on timestamp.

The Telegraf Swarm plugin collects data and creates the following series containing values, which we identified as the most interesting for Swarmk2, tags, and timestamp into InfluxDB:

- Series `swarm_node`: This series contains `cpu_shares` and `memory` as values and allow you to be grouped by `node_id` and `node_hostname` tags.
- Series `swarm`: This series contains `n_nodes` for number of nodes, `n_services` for number of services, and `n_tasks` for number of tasks. This series does not contain tags.

- Series `swarm_task_status`: This series contains number of tasks grouped by status at a time. Tags of this series are tasks status names, for example, Started, Running, and Failed.

To enable the Telegraf Swarm plugin, we will need to tweak `telegraf.conf` by adding the following configuration:

```
# Read metrics about swarm tasks and services
[[inputs.swarm]]
  # Docker Endpoint
  #    To use TCP, set endpoint = "tcp://[ip]:[port]"
  #    To use environment variables (ie, docker-machine), set endpoint =
     "ENV"
  endpoint = "unix:///var/run/docker.sock"
  timeout = "10s"
```

First, set up an instance of InfluxDB as follows:

```
$ docker run -d \
  -p 8083:8083 \
  -p 8086:8086 \
  --expose 8090 \
  --expose 8099 \
  -e PRE_CREATE_DB=telegraf \
  --name influxsrv
  tutum/influxdb
```

Then, set up an instance of Grafana, as follows:

```
docker run -d \
            -p 80:3000 \
            -e HTTP_USER=admin \
            -e HTTP_PASS=admin \
            -e INFLUXDB_HOST=$(belt ip influxdb) \
            -e INFLUXDB_PORT=8086 \
            -e INFLUXDB_NAME=telegraf \
            -e INFLUXDB_USER=root \
            -e INFLUXDB_PASS=root \
            --name grafana \
            grafana/grafana
```

After we setup an instance of Grafana, we can create the dashboard from the following JSON configuration:

```
https://objects-us-west-1.dream.io/swarm2k/swarm2k_final_grafana_dashboard.j
son
```

To connect the dashboard to InfluxDB, we will have to define the default data source and point it to the InfluxDB host port `8086`. Here's the JSON configuration to define the data source. Replace `$INFLUX_DB_IP` with your InfluxDB instance.

```
{
        "name":"telegraf",
        "type":"influxdb",
        "access":"proxy",
        "url":"http://$INFLUX_DB_IP:8086",
        "user":"root",
        "password":"root",
        "database":"telegraf",
        "basicAuth":true,
        "basicAuthUser":"admin",
        "basicAuthPassword":"admin",
        "withCredentials":false,
        "isDefault":true
}
```

After linking everything together, we'll see a dashboard like this:

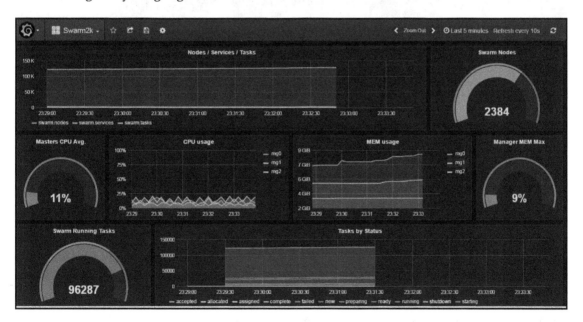

Swarm3k

Swarm3k was the second collaborative project trying to form a very large Docker cluster with the Swarm mode. It was fired up on 28th October 2016 with more than 50 individuals and companies joining this project.

Sematext was one of the very first companies that offered to help us by offering their Docker monitoring and logging solution. They became the official monitoring system for Swarm3k. Stefan, Otis, and their team provided wonderful support for us from the very beginning.

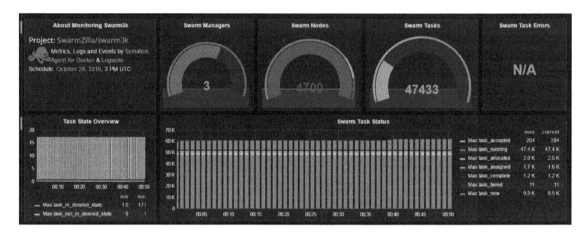

Sematext Dashboard

Sematext is the one and only Docker monitoring company that allows us to deploy the monitoring agents as the global Docker service at the moment. This deployment model provides for a greatly simplified monitoring process.

Swarm3k Setup and Workload

We aimed at 3000 nodes, but in the end, we successfully formed a working, geographically distributed 4,700-node Docker Swarm cluster.

The managers' specifications were high-mem 128GB DigitalOcean nodes in the same Data Center, each with 16 vCores.

The cluster init configuration included an undocumented "KeepOldSnapshots", which tells the Swarm mode not to delete but preserve all data snapshots for later analysis. The Docker daemon of each manager started in the DEBUG mode so to have more information on the go..

We used belt to set up the managers, as we showed in the previous section, and waited for contributors to join their workers.

Docker 1.12.3 was used on managers, while workers were a mix of 1.12.2 and 1.12.3. We organized the services on the *ingress* and *overlay* networks.

We planned the following two workloads:

- MySQL with WordPress cluster
- C1M (Container-1-Million)

25 nodes were intended to form a MySQL cluster. First, we created an overlay network, `mydb`:

```
$ docker network create -d overlay mydb
```

Then, we prepared the following `entrypoint.sh` script:

```
#!/bin/bash
ETCD_SUBNET=${ETCD_SUBNET:-10.0.0.0}
ETCD_HOST=$(ip route get $ETCD_SUBNET | awk 'NR==1 {print $NF}')
/usr/local/bin/etcd \
 -name etcd0 \
 -advertise-client-urls
   http://${ETCD_HOST}:2379,http://${ETCD_HOST}:4001 \
 -listen-client-urls http://0.0.0.0:2379,http://0.0.0.0:4001 \
 -initial-advertise-peer-urls http://${ETCD_HOST}:2380 \
 -listen-peer-urls http://0.0.0.0:2380 \
 -initial-cluster-token etcd-cluster-1 \
 -initial-cluster etcd0=http://${ETCD_HOST}:2380 \
 -initial-cluster-state new
```

Then, we will prepare a new Dockerfile for our special version of Etcd, as follows:

```
FROM quay.io/coreos/etcd
COPY entrypoint.sh /usr/local/bin/entrypoint.sh
RUN  chmod +x /usr/local/bin/entrypoint.sh
ENTRYPOINT ['/usr/local/bin/entrypoint.sh']
```

Don't forget to build it with `$ docker build -t chanwit/etcd.` before you start using it.

Third, we started an Etcd node as a central discovery service for MySQL cluster as follows:

```
$ docker service create --name etcd --network mydb chanwit/etcd
```

By inspecting the Virtual IP of Etcd, we will get the service VIP as follows:

```
$ docker service inspect etcd -f "{{ .Endpoint.VirtualIPs }}"
[{... 10.0.0.2/24}]
```

With this information, we created our `mysql` service, which can scale at any degree. Take a look at the following example:

```
docker service create \
--name mysql \
-p 3306:3306 \
--network mydb \
--env MYSQL_ROOT_PASSWORD=mypassword \
--env DISCOVERY_SERVICE=10.0.0.2:2379 \
--env XTRABACKUP_PASSWORD=mypassword \
--env CLUSTER_NAME=galera \
--mount "type=bind,src=/var/lib/mysql,dst=/var/lib/mysql" \
perconalab/percona-xtradb-cluster:5.6
```

We experienced some IP addresses issues from both mynet and ingress networks because of a Libnetwork bug; check out `https://github.com/docker/docker/issues/24637` for more information. We work around this bug by binding the cluster only to a *single* overlay network, `mydb`.

Now, we attempted a `docker service create` with the replica factor 1 for a WordPress container. We intentionally didn't control where the WordPress container would be scheduled. When we were trying to wire this WordPress service to the MySQL service, however, the connection repeatedly timed out. We concluded that for a WordPress + MySQL combo at this scale, it's much better to put a few constraints on the cluster to make all the services run together in the same data center.

Swarm performance at a scale

What you also learned from this issue was that the performance of the overlay network greatly depends on the correct tuning of network configuration on each host. As suggested by a Docker engineer, we may experience the "Neighbour Table Overflow" error when there are too many ARP requests (when the network is very big) and each host is not able to reply. These were the tunables we increased on the Docker hosts to fix the following behavior:

```
net.ipv4.neigh.default.gc_thresh1 = 30000
net.ipv4.neigh.default.gc_thresh2 = 32000
net.ipv4.neigh.default.gc_thresh3 = 32768
```

Here, `gc_thresh1` is the expected number of hosts, where `gc_thresh2` is the soft limit and `gc_thresh3` is the hard limit.

So, when the MySQL + WordPress test failed, we changed our plan to experiment NGINX on a Routing Mesh.

The ingress network was set up with a /16 pool so, it could accommodate a maximum of 64,000 IP addresses. From a suggestion by Alex Ellis, we started 4,000 (four thousands!) NGINX containers on the cluster. During this test, nodes were still coming in and out. Eventually, a few minutes later, the NGINX service started and the Routing Mesh was formed. It could correctly serve, even as some nodes kept failing, so this test verified that the Routing Mesh in 1.12.3 is rock solid and production ready.We then stopped the NGINX service and started to test the scheduling of as many containers as possible, aiming at 1,000,000, one million.

So, we created an "alpine top" service, as we did for Swarm2k. However, the scheduling rate was a bit slower this time. We reached 47,000 containers in approximately 30 minutes. Therefore, we foresaw it was going to take approximately ~10.6 hours to fill the cluster with our 1,000,000 containers.

As that was expected to take too much time, we decided to change plans again and go for 70,000 containers.

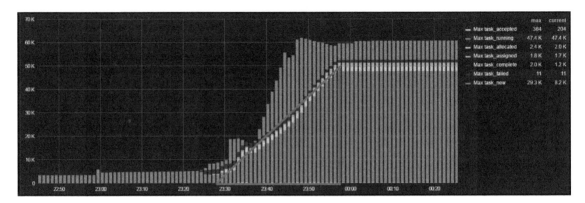

Scheduling a huge number of containers (**docker scale alpine=70000**) stressed out the cluster. This created a huge scheduling queue that would not commit until all 70,000 containers finished their scheduling. Therefore, when we decided to shut down the managers, all scheduling tasks disappeared and the cluster became unstable, for the Raft log got corrupted.

On the way, one of the most interesting things we wanted to check by collecting CPU profile information was to see what Swarm primitives were loading the cluster more.

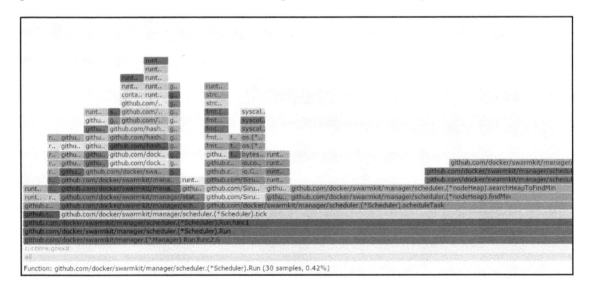

Here, we can see that only 0.42% of the CPU was spent on the scheduling algorithm. We concluded with some approximations that the Docker Swarm scheduling algorithm in version 1.12 is quite fast. This means that there is an opportunity to introduce a more sophisticated scheduling algorithm that could result in an even better resource utilization in future versions of Swarm, by adding just some acceptable overhead.

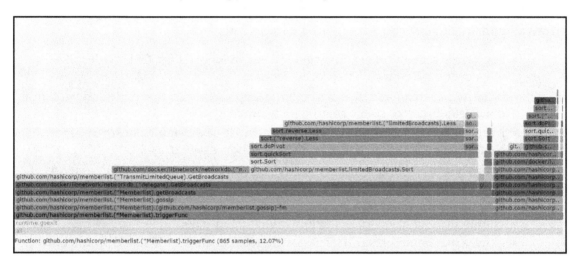

Also, we found that a lot of CPU cycles were spent on nodes communication. Here, we can see the Libnetwork member list layer. It used ~12% of the overall CPU.

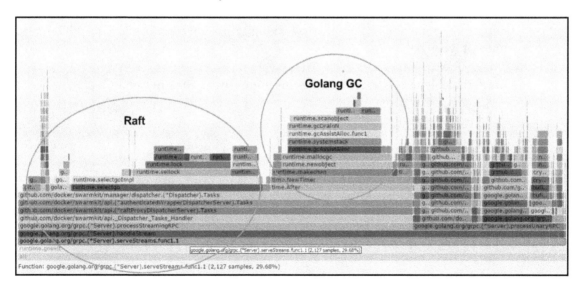

However, it seemed that the major CPU consumer was Raft, which also invoked the Go garbage collector significantly here. This used ~30% of the overall CPU.

Swarm2k and Swarm3k lessons learned

Here's a summary of what you learned from these experiments:

- For a large set of workers, managers require a lot of CPUs. CPUs will spike whenever the Raft recovery process kicks in.
- If the leading manager dies, it's better to stop Docker on that node and wait until the cluster becomes stable again with n-1 managers.
- Keep snapshot reservation as small as possible. The default Docker Swarm configuration will do. Persisting Raft snapshots uses extra CPU.
- Thousands of nodes require a huge set of resources to manage, both in terms of CPU and network bandwidth. Try to keep services and the managers' topology geographically compact.
- Hundreds of thousand tasks require high memory nodes.
- Now, a maximum of 500-1000 nodes are recommended for stable production setups.
- If managers seem to be stuck, wait; they'll recover eventually.
- The `advertise-addr` parameter is mandatory for Routing Mesh to work.
- Put your compute nodes as close to your data nodes as possible. The overlay network is great and will require tweaking Linux net configuration for all hosts to make it work best.
- Docker Swarm Mode is robust. There were no task failures, even with unpredictable network connecting this huge cluster together.

For Swarm3k, we would like to thank all the heroes: @FlorianHeigl; @jmaitrehenry from PetalMD; @everett_toews from Rackspace, Internet Thailand; @squeaky_pl, @neverlock, @tomwillfixit from Demonware; @sujaypillai from Jabil; @pilgrimstack from OVH; @ajeetsraina from Collabnix; @AorJoa and @PNgoenthai from Aiyara Cluster; @GroupSprint3r, @toughIQ, @mrnonaki, @zinuzoid from HotelQuickly; @_EthanHunt_; @packethost from Packet.io; @ContainerizeT-ContainerizeThis, The Conference; @_pascalandy from FirePress; @lucjuggery from TRAXxs; @alexellisuk; @svega from Huli; @BretFisher; @voodootikigod from Emerging Technology Advisors; @AlexPostID; @gianarb from ThumpFlow; @Rucknar, @lherrerabenitez; @abhisak from Nipa Technology; and @djalal from NexwayGroup.

We would also like to thank Sematext again for the best-of-class Docker monitoring system; and DigitalOcean for providing us with all resources.

Summary

In this chapter, we showed you how we deployed two huge Swarm clusters over Digital Ocean by using belt. These stories gave you much to learn from. We summarized the lessons and outlined some tips for running huge production swarms. On the go, we also introduced some Swarm features, such as services and security, and we discussed managers' topologies. In the next chapter, we'll discuss in detail how to administer Swarm. Topics included will be deploying workers with belt, scripts and Ansible, managing nodes, monitoring, and graphical interfaces.

5
Administer a Swarm Cluster

We're now going to see how to administer a running Swarm cluster. We will discuss in detail topics such as scaling of cluster size (adding and removing nodes), updating the cluster and node information; handling the node status (promotion and demotion), troubleshooting, and graphical interfaces (UI).

In this chapter, we will take a look at the following topics:

- Docker Swarm standalone
- Docker Swarm Mode
- Cluster management
- Swarm health
- Graphical interfaces for Swarm

Docker Swarm standalone

In standalone mode, cluster operations need to be done directly inside the container `swarm`.

In this chapter, we are not going to cover every option in detail. Swarm v1 will be deprecated soon, as it has already been declared obsolete by Swarm Mode.

```
● ● ●                          1. fsoppelsa@darthvader: ~ (zsh)
➜  ~ docker run swarm --help
Usage: swarm [OPTIONS] COMMAND [arg...]

A Docker-native clustering system

Version: 1.2.4 (5d5f7f0)

Options:
  --debug                       debug mode [$DEBUG]
  --log-level, -l "info"        Log level (options: debug, info, warn, error, fatal, panic)
  --experimental                enable experimental features
  --help, -h                    show help
  --version, -v                 print the version

Commands:
  create, c     Create a cluster
  list, l       List nodes in a cluster
  manage, m     Manage a docker cluster
  join, j       Join a docker cluster
  help          Shows a list of commands or help for one command

Run 'swarm COMMAND --help' for more information on a command.
➜  ~ █
```

The commands to administer a Docker Swarm standalone cluster are as follows:

- Create (c): As we saw in Chapter 1, *Welcome to Docker Swarm* this is how we can generate the UUID token, in case the token mechanism is going to be used. Typically, in production, people use Consul or Etcd, so this command has no relevance for production.
- List (l): This shows the list of cluster nodes based on an iteration through Consul or Etcd, that is, the Consul or Etcd must be passed as an argument.
- Join (j): Joins the node on which the swarm container is running to the cluster. Here, we need to pass a discovery mechanism at the command line.

- Manage (m): This is the core of the Standalone mode. Managing a cluster deals with changing cluster properties, such as Filters, Schedulers, external CA URLs, and timeouts. We will talk more about the application of these options to Swarm mode in `Chapter 6`, *Deploy Real Applications on Swarm* when we'll work with a real application deployment.

Docker Swarm Mode

In this section, we will continue exploring Swarm Mode commands for managing a cluster.

Manually adding nodes

You can choose to create new Swarm nodes, so Docker hosts, either way you prefer.

If Docker Machine is used, it will reach its limit very soon. You will have to be very patient while listing machines and wait for several seconds for Machine to get and print the information as a whole.

A method to add nodes manually is to use Machine with the generic driver; so, delegate host provisioning (Operating System installation, network and security groups configurations, and so on) to something else (such as Ansible), and later exploit Machine to install Docker in a proper manner. This is how it can be done:

1. Manually configure the cloud environment (security groups, networks, and so on.)
2. Provision Ubuntu hosts with a third party tool.
3. Run Machine with the generic driver on these hosts with the only goal to properly install Docker.
4. Manage hosts with the tool at part 2, or even others.

If you use Machine's generic driver, it will select the latest stable Docker binaries. While working on this book, in order to use Docker 1.12, we sometimes overcame this by giving Machine the option to get the latest unstable version of Docker with the `--engine-install-url` option:

```
docker-machine create -d DRIVER --engine-install-url
https://test.docker.com mymachine
```

At the moment of reading this book, for a production Swarm (mode), 1.12 will be stable; so this trick will not be necessary anymore, unless you need to use some of the latest Docker features.

Managers

While planning a Swarm, some considerations regarding the number of managers have to be kept in mind, as we saw in Chapter 4, *Creating a Production-Grade Swarm* . The theory of HA suggests that the number of managers must be odd and equal or more than 3. To grant a quorum in high availability means that the majority of the nodes agree on the part of node that is leading the operations.

If there are two managers and one goes down and comes back, it's possible that both will be considered leaders. This causes a logical crash in the cluster organization, which is called a split brain.

The more managers you have, the higher is the resistance ratio to failures. Take a look at the following table.

Number of managers	Quorum (majority)	Maximum possible failures
3	2	1
5	3	2
7	4	3
9	5	4

Also, in the Swarm Mode, an **ingress** overlay network is created automatically and associated to the nodes as ingress traffic. Its purpose is to be used with containers:

```
●  ●  ●                    2. fsoppelsa@yoda: ~ (zsh)

To add a manager to this swarm, run the following command:
    docker swarm join \
    --token SWMTKN-1-42mf2wtk9m5pctdqiy5bcfqorj9zlnh5n1z3sszoia7l15jwtd-bo1vg5gilk7
lvjwibtx4x0ik0 \
    192.168.99.100:2377
➜  ~ docker network ls
NETWORK ID          NAME                DRIVER              SCOPE
223104f873c6        bridge              bridge              local
8b2dcbc553f3        docker_gwbridge     bridge              local
f3ee62fb8d94        host                host                local
2qf4nt5at8xl        ingress             overlay             swarm
91f8b56fd179        none                null                local
➜  ~ █
```

You will want your containers to be associated to an internal overlay (VxLAN meshed) network to communicate with each other, rather than using public or other external networks. Thus, Swarm creates this for you and it is ready to use.

Workers number

You can add an arbitrary number of workers. This is the elastic part of the Swarm. It's totally fine to have 5, 15, 200, 2300, or 4700 running workers. This is the easiest part to handle; you can add and remove workers with no burdens, at any time, at any size.

Scripted nodes addition

The easiest way to add nodes, if you plan to not go a 100-nodes total, is to use basic scripting.

When executing `docker swarm init`, just copy-paste the lines printed as the output.

```
● ● ●                          2. fsoppelsa@yoda: ~ (zsh)
➜  ~ docker swarm init --advertise-addr 192.168.99.100
Swarm initialized: current node (c7m85xhn6ue4rx6zbb86t8rnx) is now a manager.

To add a worker to this swarm, run the following command:
    docker swarm join \
    --token SWMTKN-1-42mf2wtk9m5pctdqiy5bcfqorj9zlnh5n1z3sszoia7l15jwtd-9o4cok8
ewdszlhh8wc826ivvw \
    192.168.99.100:2377

To add a manager to this swarm, run the following command:
    docker swarm join \
    --token SWMTKN-1-42mf2wtk9m5pctdqiy5bcfqorj9zlnh5n1z3sszoia7l15jwtd-bo1vg5g
ilk7lvjwibtx4x0ik0 \
    192.168.99.100:2377
➜  ~
```

Then, create a certain bunch of workers with a loop:

```bash
#!/bin/bash
for i in `seq 0 9`; do
docker-machine create -d amazonec2 --engine-install-url
https://test.docker.com --amazonec2-instance-type "t2.large" swarm-
worker-$i
done
```

After this, it will only be necessary to go through the list of machines, `ssh` into them and `join` the nodes:

```bash
#!/bin/bash
SWARMWORKER="swarm-worker-"
for machine in `docker-machine ls --format {{.Name}} | grep
$SWARMWORKER`;
do
docker-machine ssh $machine sudo docker swarm join --token SWMTKN-
1-5c3mlb7rqytm0nk795th0z0eocmcmt7i743ybsffad5e04yvxt-
9m54q8xx8m1wa1g68im8srcme \
        172.31.10.250:2377
done
```

This script runs through the machines and for each, with a name starting with `swarm-worker-`, it will `ssh` into and join the node to the existing Swarm and to the leader manager, which is `172.31.10.250`.

 See `https://github.com/swarm2k/swarm2k/tree/master/amazonec2` for further details or to download the one liners.

Belt

Belt is another variant for provisioning Docker Engines massively. It is basically a SSH wrapper on steroids and it requires you to prepare provider-specific images as well as provision templates before `go` massively. In this section, we'll learn how to do so.

You can compile Belt yourself by getting its source from Github.

```
# Set $GOPATH here
go get https://github.com/chanwit/belt
```

Currently, Belt supports only the DigitalOcean driver. We can prepare our template for provisioning inside `config.yml`.

```
digitalocean:
        image: "docker-1.12-rc4"
        region: nyc3
        ssh_key_fingerprint: "your SSH ID"
        ssh_user: root
```

Then, we can create hundreds of nodes with a couple of commands.

First, we create three manager hosts of 16 GB each, namely `mg0`, `mg1`, and `mg2`.

```
$ belt create 16gb mg[0:2]
NAME      IPv4              MEMORY   REGION    IMAGE                    STATUS
mg2       104.236.231.136   16384    nyc3      Ubuntu docker-1.12-rc4   active
mg1       45.55.136.207     16384    nyc3      Ubuntu docker-1.12-rc4   active
mg0       45.55.145.205     16384    nyc3      Ubuntu docker-1.12-rc4   active
```

Then we can use the `status` command to wait for all nodes being active:

```
$ belt status --wait active=3
STATUS   #NODES  NAMES
active      3    mg2, mg1, mg0
```

We'll do this again for 10 worker nodes:

```
$ belt create 512mb node[1:10]
$ belt status --wait active=13

STATUS   #NODES  NAMES
active      3    node10, node9, node8, node7
```

Use Ansible

You can alternatively use Ansible (as I like, and it's becoming very popular) to make things more repeatable. We have created some Ansible modules to work with Machine and Swarm (Mode) directly; it is also compatible with Docker 1.12 (`https://github.com/fsoppelsa/a nsible-swarm`). They require Ansible 2.2+, the very first version of Ansible that is compatible with binary modules.

You will need to compile the modules (written in `go`) and then pass them to the `ansible-playbook -M` parameter.

```
git clone https://github.com/fsoppelsa/ansible-swarm
cd ansible-swarm/library
go build docker-machine.go
go build docker_swarm.go
cd ..
```

There are some example plays in playbooks. Ansible's plays syntax is so easy to understand that it is superfluous to even explain in detail.

I used this play to join 10 workers to the **Swarm2k** experiment:

```
---
name: Join the Swarm2k project
  hosts: localhost
  connection: local
  gather_facts: False
#mg0 104.236.18.183
#mg1 104.236.78.154
#mg2 104.236.87.10
  tasks:
    name: Load shell variables
```

```
shell: >
    eval $(docker-machine env "{{ machine_name }}")
    echo $DOCKER_TLS_VERIFY &&
    echo $DOCKER_HOST &&
    echo $DOCKER_CERT_PATH &&
    echo $DOCKER_MACHINE_NAME
register: worker
name: Set facts
    set_fact:
        whost: "{{ worker.stdout_lines[0] }}"
        wcert: "{{ worker.stdout_lines[1] }}"
name: Join a worker to Swarm2k
    docker_swarm:
        role: "worker"
        operation: "join"
        join_url: ["tcp://104.236.78.154:2377"]
        secret: "d0cker_swarm_2k"
        docker_url: "{{ whost }}"
        tls_path: "{{ wcert }}"
    register: swarm_result
name: Print final msg
    debug: msg="{{ swarm_result.msg }}"
```

Basically, it invokes the `docker_swarm` module after loading some host facts from Machine:

- The operation done is `join`
- The role of the new node is `worker`
- The new node joins `tcp://104.236.78.154:2377`, which was the leader manager at the moment of joining. This argument takes an array of managers, such as [`tcp://104.236.78.154:2377`, `104.236.18.183:2377`, `tcp://104.236.87.10:2377`]
- It passes the password (`secret`)
- It specifies some basic engine connection facts and the module will connect to the `dockerurl` using the certificates at `tlspath`.

After the `docker_swarm.go` is compiled in the library, joining the workers to the Swarm is as easy as:

```bash
#!/bin/bash
SWARMWORKER="swarm-worker-"
for machine in `docker-machine ls --format {{.Name}} | grep
$SWARMWORKER`;
do
ansible-playbook -M library --extra-vars "{machine_name: $machine}"
playbook.yaml
done
```

```
PLAY [Join the Swarm2k project] ******************************************

TASK [Load shell variables] *********************************************
changed: [localhost]

TASK [Set facts] ********************************************************
ok: [localhost]

TASK [Join a worker to Swarm2k] *****************************************
ok: [localhost]

TASK [Print final msg] **************************************************
ok: [localhost] => {
    "msg": "ok join"
}

PLAY RECAP *************************************************************
localhost                  : ok=4    changed=1    unreachable=0    failed=0
```

Cluster management

To illustrate cluster operations better, let's take a look at an example made up of three managers and ten workers. The first basic operation is listing nodes, with docker node ls command:

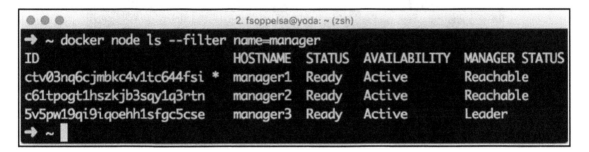

You can reference to the nodes by calling them either by their hostname (**manager1**) or by their ID (**ctv03nq6cjmbkc4v1tc644fsi**). The other columns in this list statement describes the properties of the cluster nodes.

- **STATUS** is about the physical reachability of the node. If the node is up, it's Ready, otherwise it's Down.
- **AVAILABILITY** is the node availability. A node state can either be Active (participating in the cluster operations), Pause (in standby, suspended, not accepting tasks), or Drain (waiting to be evacuated its tasks).
- **MANAGER STATUS** is the current status of manager. If a node is not the manager, this field will be empty. If a node is manager, this field can either be Reachable (one of the managers present to guarantee high availability) or Leader (the host leading all operations).

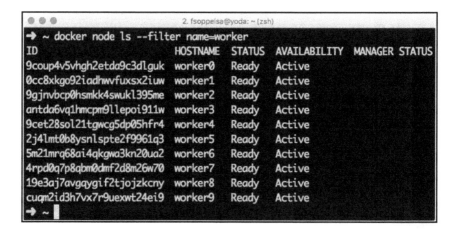

Nodes operations

The `docker node` command comes with a few possible options.

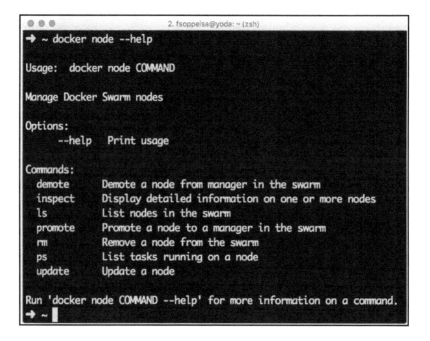

As you see, you have all the possible commands for nodes management, but `create`. We are often asked when a create option will be added to the `node` command, but there is still no answer.

So far, create new nodes is a manual operation and the responsibility of cluster operators.

Demotion and promotion

Promotion is possible for worker nodes (transforming them into managers), while demotion is possible for manager nodes (transforming them into workers).

Always remember the table to guarantee high availability when managing the a lot of managers and workers (odd number, more than or equal to three).

Use the following syntax to `promote worker0` and `worker1` to managers:

```
docker node promote worker0
docker node promote worker1
```

There is nothing magical behind the curtain. Just, Swarm attempts to change the node role with on-the-fly instructions.

ID	HOSTNAME	STATUS	AVAILABILITY	MANAGER STATUS
0cc8xkgo92iadhwvfuxsx2iuw	worker1	Ready	Active	Reachable
19e3aj7avgaygif2tjojzkcny	worker8	Ready	Active	
2j4lmt0b8ysnlspte2f9961q3	worker5	Ready	Active	
4rpd0q7p8qbm0dmf2d8m26w70	worker7	Ready	Active	
5m21mrq68ai4qkgwa3kn20ua2	worker6	Ready	Active	
5v5pw19qi9iqoehh1sfgc5cse *	manager3	Ready	Active	Reachable
9cet28sol21tgwcg5dp05hfr4	worker4	Ready	Active	
9coup4v5vhgh2etda9c3dlguk	worker0	Ready	Active	Reachable
9gjnvbcp0hsmkk4swukl395me	worker2	Ready	Active	
antda6vq1hmcpm9llepoi911w	worker3	Ready	Active	
c61tpogt1hszkjb3say1q3rtn	manager2	Ready	Active	Reachable
ctv03nq6cjmbkc4v1tc644fsi	manager1	Ready	Active	Leader
cuqm2id3h7vx7r9uexwt24ei9	worker9	Ready	Drain	

Demote is the same (docker node demote **worker1**). But be careful to avoid accidentally demoting the node you're working from, otherwise you'll get locked out.

And finally, what happens if you try to demote a Leader manager? In this case, the Raft algorithm will start an election and a new leader will be selected among the active managers.

Tagging nodes

You may have noticed, in the preceding screenshot, that **worker9** is in **Drain** availability. This means that the node is in the process of evacuating its tasks (if any), which will be rescheduled somewhere else on the cluster.

You can change node availability by updating its status, using `docker node update` command:

The availability option can be either `active`, `pause`, or `drain`. Here we just restored **worker9** to the active state.

- The `active` state means that the node is running and ready to accept tasks
- The `pause` state means that the node is running, but not accepting tasks
- The `drain` state means that the node is running and not accepting tasks, but its currently draining its tasks that are getting rescheduled somewhere else

Another powerful update argument is about labels. There are `--label-add` and `--label-rm` that allow us to add labels to Swarm nodes, respectively.

Docker Swarm labels do not affect the Engine labels. It's possible to specify labels when starting the Docker Engine (`dockerd [...] --label "staging" --label "dev" [...]`). But Swarm has no power to edit or change them. Labels we see here only affect the Swarm behavior.

Labels are useful for categorizing nodes. When you start services, you can filter and decide where to physically spawn containers, using labels. For instance, if you want to dedicate a bunch of nodes with SSD to host MySQL, you can actually:

```
docker node update --label-add type=ssd --label-add type=mysql
worker1
docker node update --label-add type=ssd --label-add type=mysql
worker2
docker node update --label-add type=ssd --label-add type=mysql
worker3
```

Later, when you will start a service with the replica factor, say three, you'll be sure that it will start MySQL containers exactly on worker1, worker2, and worker3, if you filter by `node.type`:

```
docker service create --replicas 3 --constraint 'node.type ==
mysql' --name mysql-service mysql:5.5.
```

Remove nodes

Node removal is a delicate operation. It's not just about excluding a node from the Swarm, but also about its role and the tasks it's running.

Remove workers

If a worker has the status as Down (for example, because it was physically shut down), then it's currently running nothing, so it can be safely removed:

```
docker node rm worker9
```

If a worker is in has the status as Ready, instead, then the previous command will raise an error, refusing to remove it. The node availability (Active, Pause or Drain) doesn't really matter, because it can still be potentially running tasks at the moment, or when resumed.

So, in this case an operator must manually drain the node. This means forcing it to release its tasks that will be rescheduled and moved to other workers:

```
docker node update --availability drain worker9
```

Once drained, the node can be shutdown and then removed when its status is Down.

Remove managers

Managers can't be removed. Before removing a manager node, it must be properly demoted to worker, eventually drained, and then shut down:

```
docker node demote manager3
docker node update --availability drain manager3
# Node shutdown
docker node rm manager3
```

When a manager has to be removed, another worker node should be identified as a new manager and promoted later, in order to maintain an odd number of managers.

Remove with: `docker node rm --force`
The `--force` flag removes a node, no matter what. This option must be used very carefully and it's usually the last resort in the presence of stuck nodes.

Swarm health

Swarm health depends, essentially, on the availability of the nodes in cluster and on the reliability of the managers (odd number, available, up).

Nodes can be listed with the usual:

```
docker node ls
```

This can use the `--filter` option to filter the output. For example:

```
docker node ls --filter name=manager # prints nodes named *manager*
docker node ls --filter "type=mysql" # prints nodes with a label
type tagged "mysql"
```

To get details about a specific node, use inspect as shown:

```
docker inspect worker1
```

Also, filtering options are available to extract specific data from the output JSON:

```
docker node inspect --format '{{ .Description.Resources }}' worker2
{1000000000 1044140032}
```

Outputting the number of cores (one) and the quantity of assigned memory (`1044140032` bytes, or 995M).

Backing up the cluster configuration

The important data on managers is stored in `/var/lib/docker/swarm`. Here we have:

- The certificates in `certificates/`
- The Raft status with Etcd logs and snapshots in `raft/`
- The tasks database in `worker/`
- Other less crucial information, such as the current manager status, the current connection socket, and so on.

It's a good idea to set up a periodical backup of this data, in case recovery is needed.

The space used by the Raft log depends on the number of tasks spawned onto the cluster and on how frequently their states change. For 200,000 containers, the Raft log can grow up to around 1GB of disk space every three hours. A log entry of each task occupies around 5 KB. Consequently, the log rotation policies for the Raft log directory, `/var/lib/docker/swarm/raft`, should be calibrated more or less aggressively, which depends on the available disk space.

Disaster recovery

If the swarm directory content is lost or corrupted on a manager, it's required to immediately remove that manager out of the cluster using the `docker node remove nodeID` command (and use `--force` in case it gets stuck temporarily).

The cluster administrator should not start a manager or join it to the cluster with an out-of-date swarm directory. Joining the cluster with the out-of-date swarm directory brings the cluster to an inconsistent state, as all managers will try to synchronize wrong data during the process.

After bringing down the manager with the corrupted directory, it's necessary to delete the `/var/lib/docker/swarm/raft/wal` and `/var/lib/docker/swarm/raft/snap` directories. Only after this step can the manager safely re-join the cluster.

Graphical interfaces for Swarm

At the moment of writing, Swarm mode is so young, that the existing Docker graphical user interfaces support is yet to come or is in progress.

Shipyard

Shipyard (`https://shipyard-project.com/`), which has a nice support for Swarm (v1) operations, is now updated to use Swarm mode. At the of writing (August 2016), there is a 1.12 branch on Github, that makes this workable.

At the time this book will be published, probably a stable version will be available for automated deployment already. You can take a look at the instructions at `https://shipyard-project.com/docs/deploy/automated/`.

It will be something similar to going in SSH to the leader manager host and run a one liner, such as:

```
curl -sSL https://shipyard-project.com/deploy | bash -s
```

In case we still need to install a specific non-stable branch, download it from Github to the leader manager host and install Docker Compose.

```
curl -L
https://github.com/docker/compose/releases/download/1.8.0/docker-
compose-`uname -s`-`uname -m` > /usr/local/bin/docker-compose &&
chmod +x /usr/local/bin/docker-compose
```

And finally start with `compose`:

```
docker-compose up -d < docker-compose.yml
```

This command will bring up a number of containers, which, in the very end, by default expose port 8080 so that you can connect to the public manager IP at port 8080 to get into the Shipyard UI.

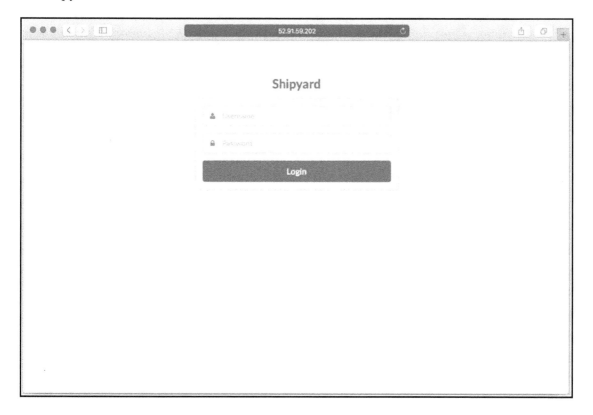

As you can see in the following screenshot, Docker Swarm features are already supported in UI (there are **Services**, **Nodes**, and so on.), and operations, such as **Promote**, **Demote**, and so on, which we outlined in this chapter are available for each node.

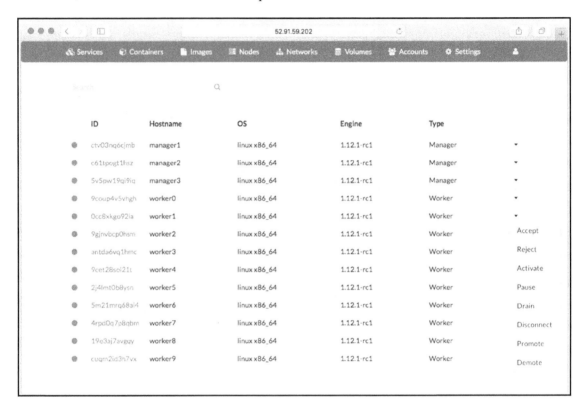

Portainer

An alternative UI supporting Swarm Mode, and our preferred choice, is **Portainer** (`https://github.com/portainer/portainer/`).

Deploying it is as easy as starting it as a container on the leader manager:

```
docker run -d -p 9000:9000 -v /var/run/:/var/run
portainer/portainer
```

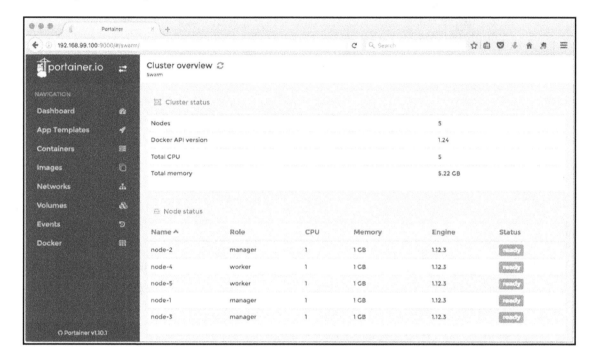

The UI has the expected options, including nice list of templates for quickly launching containers, such as MySQL or a private registry, Portainer supports Swarm services, with – s option when launching it.

Portainer, at time of writing, is about to launch the UI authentication feature, which is the first step towards full roles based access control, which is due in the start of 2017. Later the RBAC will be extended to support Microsoft Active Directory as the directory source. Further, Portainer will also support multi-cluster (or multi-host) management by end of 2016. Additional features being added at the start of 2017 are Docker Compose (YAML) support, and private registry management.

Summary

In this chapter, we went through the typical Swarm administration procedures and options. After showing how to add managers and workers to the cluster, we explained, in detail, how to update clusters and node properties, how to check the Swarm health and we encountered Shipyard and Portainer as UIs. After this we focussed on infrastructure, it's now time to use our Swarms. We'll turn the key and put in motion some real application in the next chapter, by creating real services and tasks.

6
Deploy Real Applications on Swarm

With a Swarm infrastructure we can put up various types of load to deploy. We'll work on the application stack in this and the next chapter. In this chapter we'll:

- Discover Swarm's services and tasks
- Deploy Nginx containers
- Deploy a complete WordPress
- Deploy a tiny scale Apache Spark architecture.

Microservices

The IT industry has always been keen on decoupling and reusing its creations, either source code or applications. Modeling applications at the architectural level is not an exception. Modularization was earlier called **service-oriented architecture (SOA)** and was kept glued by open source protocols based on XML. However, with the advent of containers, everyone is now speaking of micro services.

Micro services are small and self-contained autonomous modules that work together to accomplish an architectural goal.

The most inflated example of a micro service architecture is a web-application stack, for example WordPress, where web server might be one service, others being the database, cache engine, and the service containing the application itself. Modeling micro services through Docker containers can be done immediately and that's how the industry is moving ahead right now.

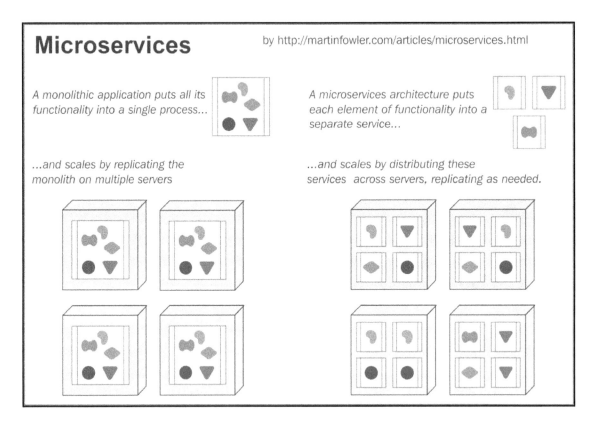

There are many advantages of using microservices and they are as follows:

- **Reusability**: You just pull the images of services you want (nginx, MySQL) in case you customize them
- **Heterogeneity**: You link existing modules embracing the different technologies. If, sometime later in the future, you decide to switch from MySQL to MariaDB, you plug off MySQL and plug in MariaDB
- **Focus on small**: Detached modules are easy to troubleshoot separately

- **Scale**: You can easily scale the web servers to 10 front ends, the cache servers to three, and architect the database replicas on five nodes, and one day scale-up or scale-down depending on the application load and needs
- **Resilience**: If you have three memcached servers and one fails, you can have mechanisms that try to resurrect it or just forget it and immediately fire up another one

Deploy a replicated nginx

We get in touch with how to use services on Swarm by starting with a simple sample: Deploy and scale Nginx.

A minimal Swarm

To make this chapter self-sufficient and useful for developers who are reading it as a stand-alone chapter. Let's quickly create a minimal Swarm Mode architecture locally, made of one manager and three workers:

1. We spawn up four Docker hosts:

   ```
   for i in seq 3; do docker-machine create -d virtualbox
   node- $i; done
   ```

2. We then take control of node-1, which we elect as our static manager, and initialize it on a Swarm:

   ```
   eval $(docker-machine env node-1)
   docker swarm init --advertise-addr 192.168.99.100
   ```

3. Docker generates a token, for us, to join our three workers. So we just copy-paste that output to iterate through the other three workers to join them to the nodes:

   ```
   for i in 2 3 4; do
   docker-machine ssh node-$i sudo docker swarm join \
   --token SWMTKN-1-
   4d1310cf5ipq7e4x5ax2akalds8j1zm6lye8knnb0ba9wftymn-
   9odd9z4gfu4d09z2iu0r2361v \
   192.168.99.100:2377
   ```

Swarm Mode architecture is always connected to `node-1` by Docker Machine-shell environment variables that are filled by the previous `eval` command. We need to check whether all the nodes, including the leader manager, are active and successfully joined to the Swarm:

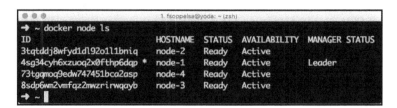

Now, we can check the status of this Swarm cluster using `docker info` command:

```
→ ~ docker info
Containers: 0
 Running: 0
 Paused: 0
 Stopped: 0
Images: 2
Server Version: 1.12.1
Storage Driver: aufs
 Root Dir: /mnt/sda1/var/lib/docker/aufs
 Backing Filesystem: extfs
 Dirs: 4
 Dirperm1 Supported: true
Logging Driver: json-file
Cgroup Driver: cgroupfs
Plugins:
 Volume: local
 Network: bridge null host overlay
Swarm: active
 NodeID: 4sg34cyh6xzuoq2x0fthp6dqp
 Is Manager: true
 ClusterID: 7675xrrjy6lr7nxvf9gdqw3v9
 Managers: 1
 Nodes: 4
 Orchestration:
  Task History Retention Limit: 5
 Raft:
  Snapshot Interval: 10000
  Heartbeat Tick: 1
  Election Tick: 3
 Dispatcher:
  Heartbeat Period: 5 seconds
 CA Configuration:
  Expiry Duration: 3 months
 Node Address: 192.168.99.100
```

The important information here is that Swarm is active, and then some Raft details follow.

Docker service

A new command introduced in Docker 1.12 is `docker service` and that's what we're going to see now. Service is the primary way by which you'll operate applications on Docker Swarm mode; it's how you will create, destroy, scale and roll update services.

Services are made of tasks. An nginx service is made-up of nginx container tasks. The service mechanism spins-up the tasks on (typically) worker nodes. So, when you create a service, you have to mandatorily specify, among its options, a service name and the container that will be the base of the service.

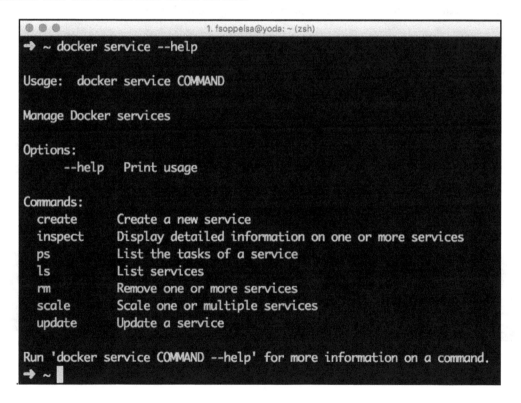

```
1. fsoppelsa@yoda: ~ (zsh)
➜ ~ docker service --help

Usage:  docker service COMMAND

Manage Docker services

Options:
      --help    Print usage

Commands:
  create    Create a new service
  inspect   Display detailed information on one or more services
  ps        List the tasks of a service
  ls        List services
  rm        Remove one or more services
  scale     Scale one or multiple services
  update    Update a service

Run 'docker service COMMAND --help' for more information on a command.
➜ ~
```

The syntax to create the services is very immediate: You just use the `docker service create` command, specifying options, such as the exposed ports, and select the container to use. Here we execute

```
docker service create -p 80:80 --name swarm-nginx --replicas 3
fsoppelsa/swarm-nginx
```

```
1. fsoppelsa@yoda: ~ (zsh)
→ ~ docker service create -p 80:80 --name swarm-nginx --replicas 3 fsoppelsa/swarm-nginx
cz7ufryb3ipvnax6ufsor5cvv
→ ~ ▊
```

This command starts nginx, exposes the container's port `80` to the host's port `80`, so that they can be reached from outside, and specifies a replica factor of three.

Replica factor is the way you scale containers on Swarm. If you specify three, Swarm will create three nginx tasks (containers) on three nodes and try to preserve this number, in case one or more of these containers die, by rescheduling nginx on other available hosts (where possible).

If a no `--replicas` option is given, then the default replica factor is `1`.

After some time, Swarm needs to pull the image from the hub, or any registry locally, to the hosts and create the appropriate container (and exposing the port); we see that three nginx are in place on our infrastructure with the command:

```
docker service ls
```

```
1. fsoppelsa@yoda: ~ (zsh)
→ ~ docker service ls
ID              NAME          REPLICAS   IMAGE                     COMMAND
cz7ufryb3ipv    swarm-nginx   3/3        fsoppelsa/swarm-nginx
→ ~ ▊
```

These tasks are actually scheduled on three nodes, as shown using the following command:

```
docker service ps swarm-nginx
```

```
● ● ●                              1. fsoppelsa@yoda: ~ (zsh)
➜  ~ docker service ps swarm-nginx
ID                          NAME            IMAGE                   NODE     DESIRED STATE  CURRENT STATE           ERROR
8gz8x07toy0gpt9yfe7crgvg6   swarm-nginx.1   fsoppelsa/swarm-nginx   node-1   Running        Running 3 minutes ago
8bwdaeecl53uuaejdzdtizhou   swarm-nginx.2   fsoppelsa/swarm-nginx   node-3   Running        Running 3 minutes ago
a7x1fr5ksl6x9m3y4wqzduyh4   swarm-nginx.3   fsoppelsa/swarm-nginx   node-4   Running        Running 3 minutes ago
➜  ~ 
```

The `fsoppelsa/swarm-nginx` container used here is a trivial modification of `richarvey/nginx-php-fpm`, which is a nginx image empowered by PHP. We used PHP to output on the Nginx welcome page the address of the current server, by adding a PHP command with the purpose of showing the load balancing mechanism.

```
<h2>Docker swarm host <?php echo $_SERVER['SERVER_ADDR']; ?></h2>
```

```
● ● ●                    1. docker exec -ti c8ca5c1740f2 bash (docker)
➜  ~ d exec -ti c8ca5c1740f2 bash
bash-4.3# cat /var/www/html/index.php

<!DOCTYPE html>
<html>
<head>
<title>Welcome to nginx!</title>
<style>
    body {
        width: 35em;
        margin: 0 auto;
        font-family: Tahoma, Verdana, Arial, sans-serif;
    }
</style>
</head>
<body>
<h1>Welcome to nginx!</h1>
<h2>Docker swarm host <?php echo $_SERVER['SERVER_ADDR']; ?></h2>
<p>If you see this page, the nginx web server is successfully installed and
working. Further configuration is required.</p>
<p><em>Thank you for using nginx.</em></p>
</body>
</html>
bash-4.3# 
```

Now if you point your browser to the manager IP and reload several times, you'll see that a load balancer is actually redirecting you to different containers sometimes.

First page that will load will be similar to the following screenshot:

The following screenshot shows another page loaded, with a different node selected by the load balancer, 10.255.0.9:

The following screenshot is of another page loaded when the load balancer redirects to node 10.255.0.10:

Overlay networks

If instead of just replicating, you want to connect containers running on different hosts to your Swarm infrastructure, you have to use networks. For example, you need to connect your web servers to your database containers so that they can communicate.

The answer to this, in Swarm Mode, is to use overlay networks. They are implemented with Docker's libnetwork and libkv. These networks are VxLAN networks built on top of another network (in the standard setup, the physical host network).

VxLAN is an extension of the VLAN protocol, aiming at increasing its scalability. Containers on different hosts, connected to Docker VxLAN networks, can communicate as if they are on the same host.

Docker Swarm Mode includes a routing mesh table that enables this multi-host networking, by default, called **ingress**.

Integrated load balancing

How does the load balancing work on Swarm Mode 1.12? The routing works in two different ways. Firstly, it works through the port exposed by the Virtual IP service. Any requests to the port are distributed among the hosts hosting the service tasks. Secondly, the service is given a Virtual IP address that is routable only inside the Docker Network. When requests are made to this VIP address, they are distributed to the underlying containers. This Virtual IP is registered inside the DNS server included in Docker Swarm. When a DNS query is done on the service name (for example nslookup mysql), the Virtual IP is returned.

Connecting services: A WordPress example

The possibility of launching a bunch of replicated and load balanced containers is already a good start, but how about more complex application stacks, made of different interconnected containers?

In this case, you can link containers by calling them by name. As we just saw, the internal Swarm DNS server will guarantee a reliable name resolution mechanism. If you instantiate a service called `nginx`, you can just reference it as `nginx` and other services will resolve to the `nginx` Virtual IP (load balanced), hence accessing the distributed containers.

To demonstrate this with an example, we're now going to deploy the more classical of classics on Swarm: WordPress. You can run WordPress as a container, in fact a ready image is available on the Docker Hub, however it requires an external database (in this case MySQL) to store its data.

So, as a start, we'll create a new dedicated overlay network on Swarm, called WordPress, and run one MySQL container on top of it as a Swarm service and three load balanced WordPress containers (web containers) also as a Swarm service. MySQL will expose port 3306, while WordPress will expose port 80.

Let's start by defining our overlay network. When connected to the Swarm manager, we issue the following command:

```
docker network create --driver overlay wordpress
```

So, what happens behind the curtain? The command creates an overlay network with libnetwork, which becomes available on the Swarm nodes when they get scheduled tasks requiring it. It will always be present if you connect to node-2 and list networks.

We now create a MySQL service, made of just one container (no MySQL native replicas nor Galera or other replication mechanisms) with the following command:

```
docker service create \
--name mysql \
--replicas 1 \
-p 3306:3306 \
--network wordpress \
--env MYSQL_ROOT_PASSWORD=dockerswarm \
mysql:5.6
```

We want to pull MySQL 5.6 from the hub, call the service (later accessible via resolved name pointing to its VIP) `mysql`, set replicas to one for clarity, expose port `3306`, specify the dedicated network WordPress, and the root password, in our case it's `dockerswarm`:

```
● ● ●                       1. fsoppelsa@yoda: ~ (zsh)
➜ ~ docker service create \
> --name mysql \
> --replicas 1 \
> -p 3306:3306 \
> --network wordpress \
> --env MYSQL_ROOT_PASSWORD=dockerswarm \
> mysql:5.6
bhzvq7tl2p85p409qp67r0i81
➜ ~ █
```

It is necessary to pull the MySQL image from the hub after a few seconds, we can check and see that in our case a `mysql` container was downloaded and placed on `node-1` (actually, masters can run containers if not specified differently), and the VIP is `10.255.0.2`, on the WordPress network. We can get this information with the following command:

```
docker service inspect mysql -f "{{ .Endpoint.VirtualIPs }}"
```

```
● ● ●                       1. fsoppelsa@yoda: ~ (zsh)
➜ ~ docker service ls
ID              NAME    REPLICAS   IMAGE        COMMAND
agqdoyh723fj    mysql   1/1        mysql:5.6
➜ ~ docker service ps mysql
ID                          NAME      IMAGE       NODE     DESIRED STATE   CURRENT STATE              ERROR
5c28bwm3detyz7eiq77zb3vca   mysql.1   mysql:5.6   node-1   Running         Running 17 seconds ago
➜ ~ d service inspect mysql -f "{{ .Endpoint.VirtualIPs }}"
[{6ha06jgn7zudgn410i5zqk0az 10.255.0.2/16} {4xl32a8cc24qq44f6d15rjdv5 10.0.0.2/24}]
➜ ~ █
```

We now have a running MySQL, we just need to launch and connect it to WordPress.

Swarm scheduling strategies

It just happened that we started a service and Swarm scheduled the container to be run on node-1. Swarm mode (as of now, at the time of writing Docker 1.12, and 1.13-dev) has only one possible strategy: spread. Spread counts the number of containers on each host and attempts to place newly created containers on the less loaded hosts (that is, hosts with less containers). Despite the fact that there is only one spread strategy available on this day, Swarm comes with options that allow us to filter the hosts, on which the tasks will be launched, with good precision.

These options are called **constraints** and may be passed as an optional argument when services are instantiated with --constraint.

We now want to start WordPress. We decide that we want to forcibly execute three containers on the three workers and not on the master, so we specify a constraint.

Constraints are of the form of --constraintnode.KEY == VALUE or --constraintnode.KEY != VALUE and there are several variants. An operator can filter by node id, role, and hostname. More interesting, as we saw in Chapter 5, *Administer a Swarm Cluster*, is the possibility to specify custom labels by adding it to the node attributes with the docker node update --label-add command.

Key	Meaning	Example
node.id	ID of node	node.id == 3tqtddj8wfyd1dl92o1l1bniq
node.role	Node role (manager, worker)	node.role != manager
node.hostname	Node hostname	node.hostname == node-1
node.labels	Labels	node.labels.type == database

Now, WordPress

Here we want to start `wordpress` on all workers, so we say that the constraint is `node.role != manager` (or `node.role == worker`). Also, we call the service, just `wordpress`, set the replica factor to 3, expose port 80, and say to WordPress that MySQL is located on host mysql (this is resolved internally in Swarm and points to the MySQL VIP):

```
docker service create \
--constraint 'node.role != manager' \
--name wordpress \
--replicas 3 \
-p 80:80 \
--network wordpress \
--env WORDPRESS_DB_HOST=mysql \
--env WORDPRESS_DB_USER=root \
--env WORDPRESS_DB_PASSWORD=dockerswarm \
wordpress
```

```
1. fsoppelsa@yoda: ~ (zsh)
➜  ~ docker service create \
> --constraint 'node.role != manager' \
> --name wordpress \
> --replicas 3 \
> -p 80:80 \
> --network wordpress \
> --env WORDPRESS_DB_HOST=mysql \
> --env WORDPRESS_DB_USER=root \
> --env WORDPRESS_DB_PASSWORD=dockerswarm \
> wordpress
14onjg4nmd06vq7dvc3a66cme
➜  ~
```

After some time, we need to download WordPress images to the workers so that we can check if everything is up and running.

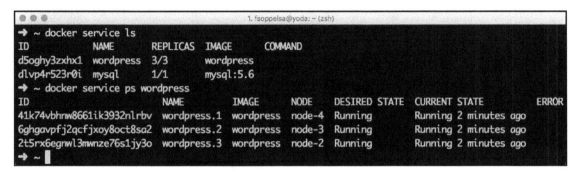

We now connect to one of the hosts on port 80 and we're welcomed by the WordPress installer.

WordPress is ready after a few steps, such as selecting an admin username and a password, are performed in the browser:

Docker Compose and Swarm mode

Many developers enjoy using Compose to model their applications, for example applications similar to WordPress. We do the same and think that it's a fantastic way to describe and manage micro services on Docker. However, at the time of writing this book, no support for Docker Swarm Mode is available in Compose yet and all containers are scheduled on the current node. To deploy an application across the swarm, we need to use the new bundle feature of stacks.

At the time of writing, stacks are available only experimentally, but we're showing them here just to give you a taste of what it will be like to deploy microservices on Docker in the (near) future.

Introducing Docker stacks

For Docker, stacks will be the standard way of packaging applications made by multiple containers. Consider the hyper inflated WordPress example: You need a minimum of one web server and one database.

Developers usually describe these applications with Compose, by creating a YAML, as shown:

```
version: '2'
services:
  db:
    image: mysql:5.6
    volumes:
      - "./.data/db:/var/lib/mysql"
    restart: always
    environment:
      MYSQL_ROOT_PASSWORD: dockerswarm
      MYSQL_DATABASE: wordpress
      MYSQL_USER: wordpress
      MYSQL_PASSWORD: wordpress
  wordpress:
    depends_on:
      - db
    image: wordpress:latest
    links:
      - db
    ports:
      - "8000:80"
    restart: always
    environment:
      WORDPRESS_DB_HOST: db:3306
      WORDPRESS_DB_PASSWORD: wordpress
```

Then, they launch this application with a command such as:

```
docker-compose --rm -d --file docker-compose.yml up.
```

Here, `mysql` and `wordpress` containers are scheduled, pulled, and started as daemons on the host to which the developer is connected. Starting from Docker 1.12 (experimental in 1.12), it will be possible to package `mysql + wordpress` in a single file package, called **Distributed Application Bundle** (**DAB**).

Distributed Application Bundles

So, instead of `docker-compose up` command, you will run:

```
docker-compose --file docker-compose.yml bundle -o wordpress.dab
```

This command will output another JSON, called `wordpress.dab`, which will be the starting point for deploying services described as Swarm services by Compose on Swarm.

For this example, the content of `wordpress.dab` looks similar to:

```
{
  "Services": {
    "db": {
      "Env": [
        "MYSQL_ROOT_PASSWORD=dockerswarm",
        "MYSQL_PASSWORD=wordpress",
        "MYSQL_USER=wordpress",
        "MYSQL_DATABASE=wordpress"
      ],
      "Image":
      "mysql@sha256:e9b0bc4b8f18429479b74b07f4
      d515f2ac14da77c146201a885c5d7619028f4d",
      "Networks": [
        "default"
      ]
    },
    "wordpress": {
      "Env": [
        "WORDPRESS_DB_HOST=db:3306",
        "WORDPRESS_DB_PASSWORD=wordpress"
      ],
      "Image":
      "wordpress@sha256:10f68e4f1f13655b15a5d0415
      3fe0a454ea5e14bcb38b0695f0b9e3e920a1c97",
      "Networks": [
        "default"
      ],
      "Ports": [
        {
          "Port": 80,
          "Protocol": "tcp"
        }
      ]
    }
  },
  "Version": "0.1"
```

Docker deploy

Starting from the generated `wordpress.dab` file, when connected to a Swarm manager, the developer can start a stack with the deploy command:

```
docker deploy --file wordpress.dab wordpress1
```

Now you will have two services called `wordpress1_wordpress` and `wordpress1_db`, conventionally following the syntax traditions of Compose.

This is a very primitive demo of what it will be. As an experimental feature, the support features in Compose are still not completely defined, but we expect it to change (even radically) in the future to meet the developer, Swarm, and Compose needs.

Another app: Apache Spark

Now that we have acquired some practice using services, we step up to the next level. We'll deploy Apache Spark on Swarm. Spark is an open source cluster computing framework from the Apache foundation, which is mainly used for data processing.

Spark may be (but not limited to) used for things, such as:

- Analysis of big data (Spark Core)
- Fast and scalable data structured console (Spark SQL)
- Streaming analytics (Spark Streaming)
- Graph processing (Spark GraphX)

Here we will focus mainly on the infrastructural part of Swarm. If you want to learn how to program or use Spark in detail, read Packt's selection of books on Spark. We suggest starting with *Fast Data Processing with Spark 2.0 – Third Edition*.

Spark is a neat and clear alternative for Hadoop, it is a more agile and efficient substitute for the complexity and magnitude of Hadoop.

The theoretical topology of Spark is immediate and can reckon the Swarm mode on one or more managers leading the cluster operations and a certain number of workers who are executing real tasks.

As for managers, Spark can use its own managers called standalone managers (as we'll do here) or use Hadoop YARN or even exploit Mesos features.

Then, Spark can delegate storage to an internal HDFS (Hadoop Distributed Filesystem) or to external storage services, such as Amazon S3, OpenStack Swift, or Cassandra. Storage is used by Spark to get data to elaborate and then to save the elaborated results.

Why Spark on Docker

We'll show you how to start a Spark cluster on a Docker Swarm cluster, as an alternative to start Spark with virtual machines. The example defined in this chapter can get many benefits from containers:

- Starting containers is much more quicker
- Scaling containers in a pet model is more immediate
- You can get Spark images without having to create VMs, to write custom scripts, adapt Ansible Playbooks. Just `docker pull`
- You can create a dedicated overlay network with Docker Networking features, without physically compromising or invoking a networking team

Spark standalone without Swarm

Let's start defining a tiny Apache Spark cluster built with the classical Docker tools, which are basically Docker commands on a Docker host. Before understanding the big picture, we need to start familiarizing ourselves with Swarm concepts and terminologies on the field.

In this chapter, we'll work with the `google_container` images, specifically with Swarm version 1.5.2. Many improvements are included in the 2.0 version, but these images are proven to be very stable and reliable. So, we can start by pulling them for the master and the workers from the Google repository:

```
docker pull gcr.io/google_containers/spark-master
docker pull gcr.io/google_containers/spark-worker
```

Spark can run on the top of YARN, Mesos, or Hadoop. In the following examples and chapters, we're going to use its standalone mode, because it is the easiest and requires no additional prerequisites. In a standalone Spark cluster mode, Spark allocates resources based on cores. By default, an application will grab all the cores in the cluster, so we're going to limit the resources dedicated to the workers.

Our architecture will be very straightforward: one master, which will be responsible for managing the cluster, and three workers for the nodes running Spark jobs. For our purpose, the master has to publish port `8080` (the Web UI we'll use for convenience) and we'll call it spark-master. By default, the worker containers attempt to connect to the URL `spark://spark-master:7077`, so apart from linking them to the master, no further customization are required.

So, let's pass it to the practical part and initialize a Spark master with the following code:

```
docker run -d \
-p 8080:8080 \
--name spark-master \
-h spark-master \
gcr.io/google_containers/spark-master
```

This runs in the daemon mode (-d), a container from the
`gcr.io/google_containers/spark-master` image, assigns the name (--name) spark-master to the container and configures its hostname (-h) to spark-master.

We can connect now a browser to the Docker host, at port 8080, to verify that Spark is up and running.

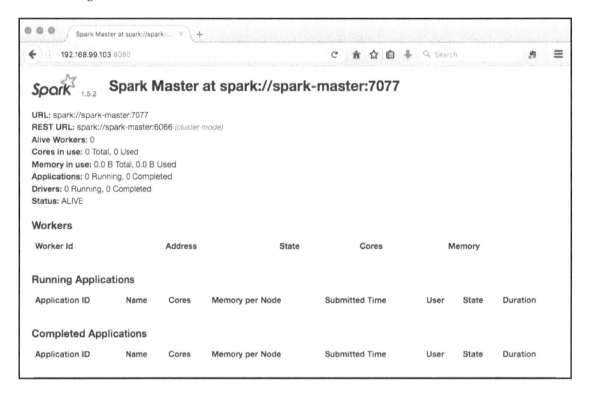

It still has no Alive Workers, which we're going to spawn now. We start the workers with the following commands just before we take note of the ID of the Spark master container:

```
docker run -d \
--link 7ff683727bbf \
-m 256 \
-p 8081:8081 \
--name worker-1 \
gcr.io/google_containers/spark-worker
```

This starts a container in the daemon mode, links it to the master, limits the memory-in-use to a maximum of 256M, exposes port 8081 to web (worker) management, and assigns it to the container name `worker-1`. Similarly, we start the other two workers:

```
docker run -d --link d3409a18fdc0 -m 256 -p 8082:8082 -m 256m --
name worker-2 gcr.io/google_containers/spark-worker
docker run -d --link d3409a18fdc0 -m 256 -p 8083:8083 -m 256m --
name worker-3 gcr.io/google_containers/spark-worker
```

We can check on the master if everything is connected and running:

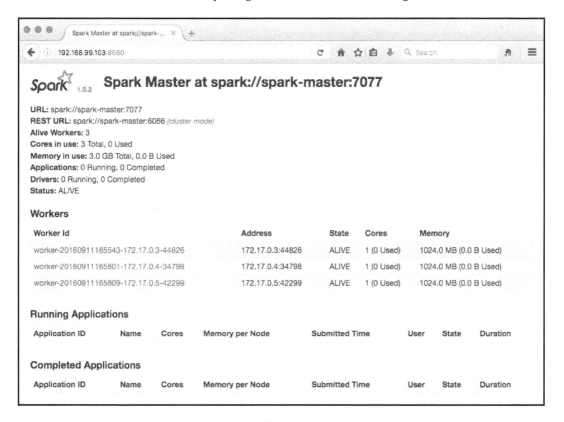

Spark standalone on Swarm

So far, we have discussed the not so important part. We're now going now to transfer the concepts already discussed to Swarm architecture, so we'll instantiate the Spark master and workers as Swarm services, instead of single containers. We'll create an architecture with a replica factor of one for the master, and a replica factor of three for the workers.

Spark topology

In this example, we'll create a Spark cluster made of one master and three workers.

Storage

We'll define a real storage and start some real Spark tasks in `Chapter 7`, *Scaling Up Your Platform*.

Prerequisites

We begin by creating a new dedicated overlay network for Spark:

```
docker network create --driver overlay spark
```

Then, we set some labels onto nodes to be able to filter later. We want to host the Spark master on the Swarm manager (`node-1`) and Spark workers on Swarm workers (node-2, 3 and 4):

```
docker node update --label-add type=sparkmaster node-1
docker node update --label-add type=sparkworker node-2
docker node update --label-add type=sparkworker node-3
docker node update --label-add type=sparkworker node-4
```

> We're adding here the 'sparkworker' type tags for extreme clarity. With only two variants, it's possible in fact to write the same constraint as:
> –constraint 'node.labels.type == sparkworker'
> Or:
> –constraint 'node.labels.type != sparkmaster'

Start Spark on Swarm

We will now define our Spark services in Swarm, similar to what we did for WordPress in the preceding section, but this time we will drive the scheduling strategy by defining where to start the Spark master and the Spark workers with the maximum precision.

We begin with the master as shown:

```
docker service create \
--container-label spark-master \
--network spark \
--constraint 'node.labels.type==sparkmaster' \
--publish 8080:8080 \
--publish 7077:7077 \
--publish 6066:6066 \
--name spark-master \
--replicas 1 \
--limit-memory 1024 \
gcr.io/google_containers/spark-master
```

A Spark master exposes port 8080 (the web UI) and optionally, for the clarity of the example, here we also expose port 7077 used by the Spark workers to connect to the master and port 6066, the Spark API port. Also, we limit the memory to 1G with –limit-memory. Once the Spark master is up, we can create the service hosting the workers, sparkworker:

```
docker service create \
--constraint 'node.labels.type==sparkworker' \
--network spark \
--name spark-worker \
--publish 8081:8081 \
--replicas 3 \
--limit-memory 256 \
gcr.io/google_containers/spark-worker
```

Similarly, we expose port `8081` (the workers web UI), but it's optional. Here, all the Spark containers are scheduled on spark worker nodes, as we defined earlier. It will take some time to pull the images to the hosts. As a result, we have the minimal Spark infrastructure:

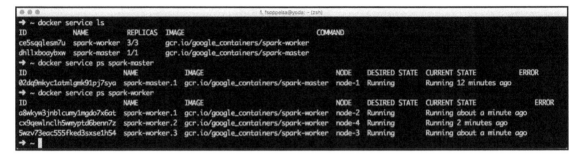

The Spark cluster is up and running, even if there is a little note to add:

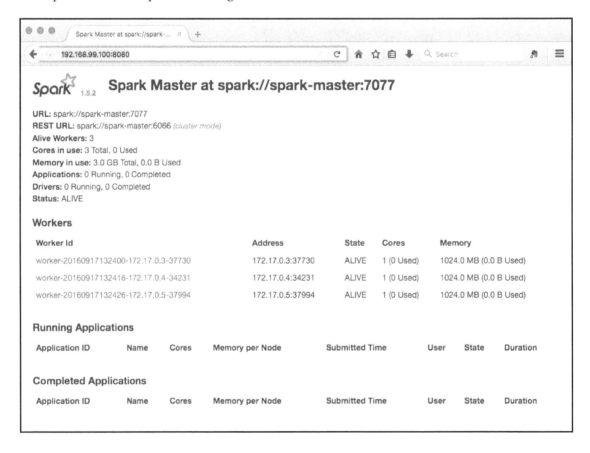

Despite the fact that we limited the memory to 256M for each worker, in the UI we still see that Spark reads 1024M. This is because of the Spark internal default configuration. If we connect to any of the hosts, where one of the workers is running, and check its statistics with the `docker stats a7a2b5bb3024` command, we see that the container is actually limited:

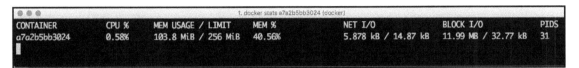

Summary

In this chapter, we started working on the application stack and deploying real things on Swarm. We did some practice in defining Swarm services and we launched a cluster of nginx, as well as a load-balanced WordPress on a dedicated overlay network. Then, we moved on to something more real: Apache Spark. We deployed Spark on Swarm at a small scale, by defining our own scheduling strategies. We are going to expand Swarm and scale it to a bigger size, with more real storage and networking options, in Chapter 7, *Scaling Up Your Platform*.

7
Scaling Up Your Platform

In this chapter, we're going to extend what we saw in Chapter 6, *Deploy Real Applications on Swarm*. Our goal is to deploy a realistic production-grade Spark cluster on top of Swarm, add storage capacity, launch some Spark jobs and setup monitoring for the underlying infrastructure.

In order to do that, this chapter is mostly infrastructure-oriented. In fact, we'll see how to coalesce **Libnetwork**, **Flocker**, and **Prometheus** with Swarm.

For network, we'll use the basic Docker Network overlay system, based on Libnetwork. There are a few great networking plugins out there, such as Weave and others, but either they are not compatible with the new Docker Swarm Mode yet, or they are made obsolete by Swarm-integrated routing mesh mechanisms.

For storage, the situation is more prosperous, because there is much more choice (refer to https://docs.docker.com/engine/extend/plugins/). We'll go with Flocker. Flocker is the *grandfather* of Docker storage, and can be configured with a vast plethora of storage backends, making it one of the best choices for production loads. Scared by Flocker complexity? Unjustified: We'll see how to set up a multiple nodes Flocker cluster for any usage, in minutes.

For monitoring, finally, we'll introduce Prometheus. It's the most promising among the monitoring systems available for Docker nowadays, and its APIs may be integrated into the Docker engine very soon.

So, what we'll cover here:

- A Spark example over Swarm, ready for running any Spark job
- Automate the installation of Flocker for infrastructures at a scale
- Demonstrate how to use Flocker locally
- Use Flocker with Swarm Mode
- Scale our Spark app
- Monitor the health of this infrastructure with Prometheus

The Spark example, again

We're going to rearchitect the example of Chapter 6, *Deploy Real Applications on Swarm*, so we'll deploy Spark on Swarm, but this time with a realistic networking and storage setup.

Spark storage backend usually runs on Hadoop, or on NFS when on filesystem. For jobs not requiring storage, Spark will create local data on workers, but for storage computations, you will need a shared filesystem on each node, which cannot be guaranteed automatically by Docker volume plugins (at least, so far).

A possibility to achieve that goal on Swarm is to create NFS shares on each Docker host, and then mount them transparently inside service containers.

Our focus here is not to illustrate Spark job details and their storage organization, but to introduce an opinionated storage option for Docker and give an idea of how to organize and scale a fairly-complex service on Docker Swarm.

Docker plugins

For a detailed introduction on Docker plugins, we can suggest to read the official documentation pages. Here is a starting point https://docs.docker.com/engine/extend /and, also, Docker will probably release a tool to get plugins with a single command, refer to https://docs.docker.com/engine/reference/commandline/plugin_install/.

We recommend you to refer to *Extending Docker* book, Packt, if you want to explore how to integrate new features into Docker. The book emphasis is on Docker plugins, volume plugins, network plugins, and how to create your own plugins.

For Flocker, **ClusterHQ** made available an automated deployment mechanism to deploy a Flocker cluster on AWS with **CloudForm** templates, which you can install using the **Volume Hub**. For registering and starting such a cluster, go to `https://flocker-docs.clu sterhq.com/en/latest/docker-integration/cloudformation.html`. For a step-by-step explanation of the detailed procedure, refer to Chapter 3 of *Extending Docker*, Packt.

Here we'll go manually, because we must integrate Flocker and Swarm.

The lab

In this tutorial, we'll create the infrastructure on AWS. Ideally, for a production environment, you would setup three or five Swarm managers and some workers, and eventually add new worker nodes later depending on the load.

Here we'll setup a Swarm cluster with three Swarm managers, six Swarm workers and one Flocker control node with Machine, and won't add new workers.

Installing Flocker requires several manual steps, which can be automated (as we'll see). So, to make the example as less complex as possible, we'll run all these commands initially, in linear order, without repeating procedures to increase the system capacity.

If you don't like Ansible, you can easily adapt the flow to your favorite tool, be it **Puppet**, **Salt**, **Chef** or others.

A unique key

For simplicity, we will install our lab using an SSH key generated ad hoc, and we'll install Docker Machines with this key copied to the host in `authorized_keys`. The goal is to have a unique key to authenticate Ansible later, that we'll use to automate the many steps that we should otherwise perform manually.

So, we start by generating a `flocker` key and we'll put it into the `keys/` directory:

```
ssh-keygen -t rsa -f keys/flocker
```

Docker Machine

To provision our Docker hosts, we'll go with Docker Machine. These are the system details for this tutorial:

AWS instances will be called from aws-101 to aws-110. This standardized naming will be important later when we'll need to generate and create node certificates for Flocker:

- Nodes aws-101, 102, 103 will our Swarm managers
- Node aws-104 will be the Flocker control node
- Nodes from aws-105 to aws-110 will be our Swarm workers.

The instance type will be `t2.medium` (2 vCPUs, 4G memory, EBS storage)

The flavor will be Ubuntu 14.04 Trusty (specified with the `--amazonec2-ami` parameter)

The security group will be the standard `docker-machine` (we'll summarize the requirements again in a few seconds)

The Flocker version will be 1.15.

The exact AMI ID to use can be searched on `https://cloud-images.ubuntu.com/locator/ec2/`.

The AWS calculator computes this setup's cost to roughly 380$ monthly, storage usage excluded.

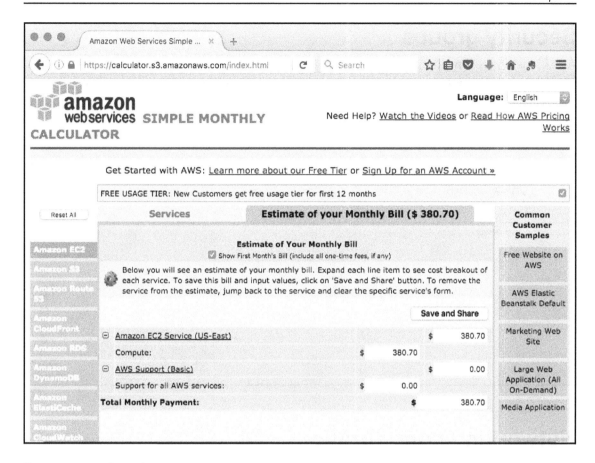

So, we create the infrastructure:

```
for i in `seq 101 110`; do
docker-machine create -d amazonec2 \
--amazonec2-ami ami-c9580bde \
--amazonec2-ssh-keypath keys/flocker \
--amazonec2-instance-type "t2.medium" \
aws-$i;
done
```

and running.

After some time, we'll have it up and running.

Security groups

Additionally, we'll need open three additional new ports in the security Group used for this project (`docker-machine`) in the EC2 console. There are ports used by Flocker services:

- Port `4523/tcp`
- Port `4524/tcp`

Also, the following is a port used by Swarm:

- Port `2377/tcp`

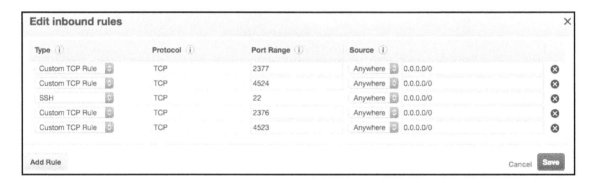

Networking configuration

We use a standard configuration with an additional overlay network, called **Spark**. Traffic data will pass through the spark network, making it possible to extend the lab configuration with new hosts and workers running even on other providers, such as **DigitalOcean** or **OpenStack**. When new Swarm workers join this cluster, this network is propagated to them and made available for Swarm services.

Storage configuration and architecture

As mentioned, we chose Flocker (`https://clusterhq.com/flocker/introduction/`), which is among the top Docker storage projects. ClusterHQ describes it as:

Flocker is an open-source container data volume manager for your Dockerized applications. By providing tools for data migrations, Flocker gives the ops teams the tools they need to run containerized stateful services such as databases in production.
Unlike a Docker data volume that is tied to a single server, a Flocker data volume, called a dataset, is portable and can be used with any container in your cluster.

Flocker supports a very wide set of storage options, from AWS EBS to EMC, NetApp, Dell, Huawei solutions, to OpenStack Cinder and Ceph, just to mention some.

Its design is straightforward: Flocker has a **control node**, which exposes its service APIs to manage the Flocker cluster and Flocker volumes, and a **Flocker Agent** alongside with the Docker plugin runs on each **node** of the cluster.

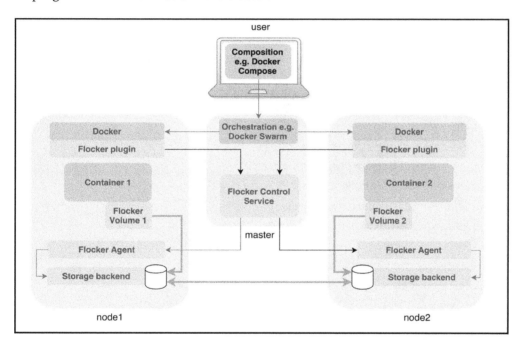

To use Flocker, at the command line, you would need to run something like this with Docker to read or write stateful data on a Flocker `myvolume` volume mounted as `/data` inside the container:

```
docker run -v myvolume:/data --volume-driver flocker image command
```

Also, you can manage volume with the `docker volume` command:

```
docker volume ls
docker volume create -d flocker
```

In this tutorial architecture, we'll install the Flocker control node on aws-104, that will be hence dedicated, and flocker agents on all nodes (node-104 included).

Also, we'll install the Flocker client that used to interact with the Flocker control node APIs in order to manage the cluster status and volumes. For our convenience, we'll also use it from aws-104.

Installing Flocker

A series of operations are necessary to get a running Flocker cluster:

1. Install the `flocker-ca` utility to generate certificates.
2. Generate the authority certificate.
3. Generate the control node certificate.
4. Generate the node certificates, one per node.
5. Generate the flocker plugin certificate.
6. Generate the client certificate.
7. Install some software from packages.
8. Distribute certificates to the Flocker cluster.
9. Configure the installation, adding the main configuration file, `agent.yml`.
10. Configure the packet filter on hosts.
11. Start and restart system services.

You can execute them manually on a small cluster, but they are repetitive and tedious, so we'll illustrate the procedure using some self-explanatory Ansible playbooks published to `https://github.com/fsoppelsa/ansible-flocker`.

These plays are trivial and probably not production ready. There are also the official ClusterHQ playbooks for Flocker roles (refer to `https://github.com/ClusterHQ/ansible-role-flocker`), but for the linearity of the explanation, we'll use the first repository, so let's clone it:

```
git clone git@github.com:fsoppelsa/ansible-flocker.git
```

Generating Flocker certificates

For certificate generation, the `flocker-ca` utility is required. Instructions on how to install it are available at
`https://docs.clusterhq.com/en/latest/flocker-standalone/install-client.html`. For Linux distributions, it's a matter of installing a package. On Mac OS X, instead, the tool can be pulled using Python's `pip` utility.

On Ubuntu:

```
sudo apt-get -y install --force-yes clusterhq-flocker-cli
```

On Mac OS X:

```
pip install https://clusterhq-
archive.s3.amazonaws.com/python/Flocker-1.15.0-py2-none-any.whl
```

Once in possess of this tool, we generate the required certificates. To make the things simple, we'll create the following certificate structure:

A directory `certs/` including all certificates and keys:

- `cluster.crt` and `.key` are the authority certificate and key
- `control-service.crt` and `.key` are the control node certificate and key
- `plugin.crt` and `.key` are the Docker Flocker plugin certificate and key
- `client.crt` and `.key` are the Flocker client certificate and key
- From `node-aws-101.crt` and `.key` to `node-aws-110.crt` and `.key` are the node certificates and keys, one per node

The following are the steps:

1. Generate the authority certificate: `flocker-ca initialize cluster`
2. Once in possess of the authority certificate and key, generate the control node certificate in the same directory: `flocker-ca create-control-certificate aws-101`
3. Then generate the plugin certificate: `flocker-ca create-api-certificate plugin`
4. Then generate the client certificate: `flocker-ca create-api-certificate client`
5. Finally, generate each nodes' certificate: `flocker-ca create-node-certificate node-aws-X`

Of course, we must cheat and use the `utility/generate_certs.sh` script available in the `ansible-flocker` repository, which will do the work for us:

```
cd utils
./generate_certs.sh
```

After this script execution, we now have all our certificates available in `certs/`:

```
● ● ●        1. fsoppelsa@darthvader: ~/Projects/ansible-flocker/utils (zsh)
(flocker-client)→  utils git:(master) x ./generate_certs.sh
(flocker-client)→  utils git:(master) x ls -l certs
total 112
-rw-------  1 fsoppelsa staff 1846 Nov  1 15:07 client.crt
-rw-------  1 fsoppelsa staff 3272 Nov  1 15:07 client.key
-rw-------  1 fsoppelsa staff 1948 Nov  1 15:07 cluster.crt
-rw-------  1 fsoppelsa staff 3272 Nov  1 15:07 cluster.key
-rw-------  1 fsoppelsa staff 1874 Nov  1 15:07 control-service.crt
-rw-------  1 fsoppelsa staff 3272 Nov  1 15:07 control-service.key
-rw-------  1 fsoppelsa staff 1854 Nov  1 15:07 node-aws-101.crt
-rw-------  1 fsoppelsa staff 3268 Nov  1 15:07 node-aws-101.key
-rw-------  1 fsoppelsa staff 1854 Nov  1 15:07 node-aws-102.crt
-rw-------  1 fsoppelsa staff 3272 Nov  1 15:07 node-aws-102.key
-rw-------  1 fsoppelsa staff 1854 Nov  1 15:07 node-aws-103.crt
-rw-------  1 fsoppelsa staff 3272 Nov  1 15:07 node-aws-103.key
-rw-------  1 fsoppelsa staff 1854 Nov  1 15:07 node-aws-104.crt
-rw-------  1 fsoppelsa staff 3272 Nov  1 15:07 node-aws-104.key
-rw-------  1 fsoppelsa staff 1854 Nov  1 15:07 node-aws-105.crt
-rw-------  1 fsoppelsa staff 3272 Nov  1 15:07 node-aws-105.key
-rw-------  1 fsoppelsa staff 1854 Nov  1 15:07 node-aws-106.crt
-rw-------  1 fsoppelsa staff 3272 Nov  1 15:07 node-aws-106.key
-rw-------  1 fsoppelsa staff 1854 Nov  1 15:07 node-aws-107.crt
-rw-------  1 fsoppelsa staff 3276 Nov  1 15:07 node-aws-107.key
-rw-------  1 fsoppelsa staff 1854 Nov  1 15:07 node-aws-108.crt
-rw-------  1 fsoppelsa staff 3272 Nov  1 15:07 node-aws-108.key
-rw-------  1 fsoppelsa staff 1854 Nov  1 15:07 node-aws-109.crt
-rw-------  1 fsoppelsa staff 3268 Nov  1 15:07 node-aws-109.key
-rw-------  1 fsoppelsa staff 1854 Nov  1 15:07 node-aws-110.crt
-rw-------  1 fsoppelsa staff 3276 Nov  1 15:07 node-aws-110.key
-rw-------  1 fsoppelsa staff 1846 Nov  1 15:07 plugin.crt
-rw-------  1 fsoppelsa staff 3272 Nov  1 15:07 plugin.key
(flocker-client)→  utils git:(master) x ▮
```

Installing software

On each Flocker node, we must perform the following steps:

1. Add the ClusterHQ Ubuntu repository to the APT source list.
2. Update the packages cache.
3. Install these packages:
   - `clusterhq-python-flocker`
   - `clusterhq-flocker-node`
   - `clusterhq-flocker-docker-plugin`

4. Create a directory `/etc/flocker`.
5. Copy the Flocker configuration file `agent.yml` to `/etc/flocker`.
6. Copy the certificates appropriate for that node to `/etc/flocker`.
7. Configure security by enabling **ufw**, and opening TCP ports `2376`, `2377`, `4523`, `4524`.
8. Start the system services.
9. Restart the docker daemon.

Once again, we love the machines to work for us, so let's setup this with Ansible while we have a coffee.

But, before, we must specify who will be the Flocker control node and who the bare nodes, so we fill in the `inventory` file with the host IPs of nodes. The file is in `.ini` format, and what's required is just to specify the list of nodes:

```
1. fsoppelsa@darthvader: ~/Projects/ansible-flocker (zsh)
→ ansible-flocker git:(master) x cat inventory
[control]
54.84.176.7

[nodes]
52.201.238.46
52.201.237.95
54.174.70.59
54.164.97.79
52.90.94.170
54.205.4.101
52.201.246.134
54.89.10.179
54.89.161.189
→ ansible-flocker git:(master) x █
```

Then, we create the directory from where Ansible will take files, certificates, and configurations to copy to the nodes:

```
mkdir files/
```

We now copy all our certificates we created previously, from the `certs/` directory to `files/`:

```
cp certs/* files/
```

Finally, we define the Flocker configuration file in `files/agent.yml` with the following content, adapting the AWS region and modifying `hostname`, `access_key_id`, and `secret_access_key`:

```
control-service:
    hostname: "<Control node IP>"
    port: 4524
dataset:
    backend: "aws"
    region: "us-east-1"
    zone: "us-east-1a"
    access_key_id: "<AWS-KEY>"
    secret_access_key: "<AWS-ACCESS-KEY>"
version: 1
```

This is the core Flocker configuration file, which will be in `/etc/flocker` on every node. Here, you specify and configure the credentials of the backend of choice. In our case, we go with the basic AWS option, EBS, so we include our AWS credentials.

With inventory, `agent.yml` and all certificates ready in `files/`, we can proceed.

Installing the control node

The playbook to install the control node is `flocker_control_install.yml`. This play executes a software installation script, copies the cluster certificate, the control node certificate and key, the node certificate and key, the client certificate and key, the plugin certificate and key, configures the firewall opening ports for SSH, Docker and Flocker, and starts these system services:

- `flocker-control`
- `flocker-dataset-agent`
- `flocker-container-agent`
- `flocker-docker-plugin`

Finally, it refreshes the `docker` service, restarting it.

Let's run it:

```
$ export ANSIBLE_HOST_KEY_CHECKING=False
$ ansible-playbook \
-i inventory \
--private-key keys/flocker \
playbooks/flocker_control_install.yml
```

Installing the cluster nodes

Similarly, we install the other nodes with another playbook, `flocker_nodes_install.yml`:

```
$ ansible-playbook \
-i inventory \
--private-key keys/flocker \
playbooks/flocker_nodes_install.yml
```

The steps are more or less the same as before, except that this playbook doesn't copy some certificates and doesn't start the `flocker-control` service. Only the Flocker agent and Flocker Docker plugin services run there. We wait for some time until Ansible exits.

```
● ● ●                    1. fsoppelsa@darthvader: ~/Projects/ansible-flocker (zsh)
✕ ..sible-flocker (zsh) 🔋 ⌘1   ✕ root@aws-104: ~ (do... ⌘2   ✕      ~ (zsh)      🔋 ⌘3
PLAY RECAP *********************************************************************
52.201.237.95              : ok=7    changed=5    unreachable=0    failed=0
52.201.238.46              : ok=7    changed=5    unreachable=0    failed=0
52.201.246.134             : ok=7    changed=5    unreachable=0    failed=0
52.90.94.170               : ok=7    changed=5    unreachable=0    failed=0
54.164.97.79               : ok=7    changed=5    unreachable=0    failed=0
54.174.70.59               : ok=7    changed=5    unreachable=0    failed=0
54.205.4.101               : ok=7    changed=5    unreachable=0    failed=0
54.89.10.179               : ok=7    changed=5    unreachable=0    failed=0
54.89.161.189              : ok=7    changed=5    unreachable=0    failed=0

→  ansible-flocker git:(master) ✗ █
```

Testing whether everything is up and running

To check that Flocker is installed correctly, we now log in to the control node, check that the Flocker plugin is running (alas, it has the `.sock` file), and then we install the `flockerctl` utility (refer to

`https://docs.clusterhq.com/en/latest/flocker-features/flockerctl.html`) with the `curl` command:

```
$ docker-machine ssh aws-104
$ sudo su -
# ls /var/run/docker/plugins/flocker/
flocker.sock   flocker.sock.lock
# curl -sSL https://get.flocker.io |sh
```

We now set some environment variables used by `flockerctl`:

```
export FLOCKER_USER=client
export FLOCKER_CONTROL_SERVICE=54.84.176.7
export FLOCKER_CERTS_PATH=/etc/flocker
```

We can now list the nodes and volumes (we still have no volumes yet, of course):

```
flockerctl status
flockerctl list
```

```
● ● ●                    2. root@aws-104: ~ (docker-machine)
root@aws-104:~# export FLOCKER_USER=client
root@aws-104:~# export FLOCKER_CONTROL_SERVICE=54.84.176.7
root@aws-104:~# export FLOCKER_CERTS_PATH=/etc/flocker
root@aws-104:~# flockerctl status
SERVER      ADDRESS
7df66dfd    172.31.5.7
409c3deb    172.31.2.37
885e9b3a    172.31.3.98
27bdd502    172.31.8.178
59430473    172.31.1.35
c12bfac9    172.31.6.150
e651fc75    172.31.8.52
d8759beb    172.31.0.213
05d393e4    172.31.8.38
63e67423    172.31.0.30

root@aws-104:~# flockerctl list
DATASET    SIZE    METADATA    STATUS    SERVER

root@aws-104:~# ▮
```

Now, we can go to another node of the cluster to check the connectivity of the Flocker cluster (especially if the plugin and the agent can reach and authenticate to the control node), say `aws-108`, create a volume and write some data into it:

```
$ docker-machine ssh aws-108
$ sudo su -
# docker run -v test:/data --volume-driver flocker \
busybox sh -c "echo example > /data/test.txt"
# docker run -v test:/data --volume-driver flocker \
busybox sh -c "cat /data/test.txt"
example
```

```
● ● ●                          3. root@aws-108: ~ (docker-machine)
root@aws-108:~# docker volume ls
DRIVER          VOLUME NAME
root@aws-108:~# docker run -v test:/data --volume-driver flocker busybox sh -c "echo example > /data/test.txt"
root@aws-108:~# docker run -v test:/data --volume-driver flocker busybox sh -c "cat /data/test.txt"
example
root@aws-108:~# 
```

If we go back to the control node, `aws-104`, we can verify that volumes with persistent data got created by listing them with the docker and `flockerctl` commands:

```
docker volume ls
flockerctl list
```

```
● ● ●                          2. root@aws-104: ~ (docker-machine)
root@aws-104:~# docker volume ls
DRIVER          VOLUME NAME
flocker         test
root@aws-104:~# flockerctl list
DATASET                                    SIZE    METADATA    STATUS        SERVER
8577ed21-25a0-4c68-bafa-640f664e774e       75.00G  name=test   attached ☑    7df66dfd (172.31.5.7)

root@aws-104:~# 
```

Excellent! So now we can remove the exited containers, delete the test volume dataset from Flocker, and then we are ready to install a Swarm:

```
# docker rm -v ba7884944577
# docker rm -v 7293a156e199
# flockerctl destroy -d 8577ed21-25a0-4c68-bafa-640f664e774e
```

Installing and configuring Swarm

We can now install a Swarm with our favorite method, as shown in the previous chapters. We'll have **aws-101** to **aws-103** as managers, and the rest of nodes except **aws-104**, workers. This cluster can be expanded even further. For practical things, we'll keep it at 10-nodes size.

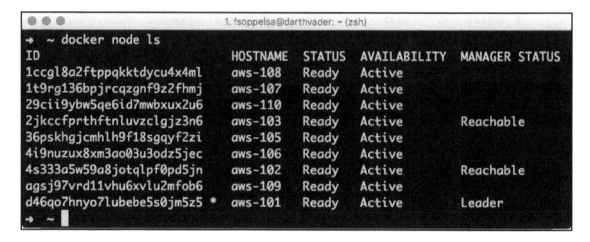

We now add a dedicated `spark` overlay VxLAN network:

```
docker network create --driver overlay --subnet 10.0.0.0/24 spark
```

A volume for Spark

We now connect to any Docker host and create a `75G` sized volume to be used to save some persistent Spark data:

```
docker volume create -d flocker -o size=75G -o profile=bronze --
name=spark
```

The option to discuss here is `profile`. This is a sort of flavor of storage (speed, mostly). As explained in the link `https://docs.clusterhq.com/en/latest/flocker-features/aws-configuration.html#aws-dataset-backend`, ClusterHQ maintains three available profiles for AWS EBS:

- **Gold**: EBS Provisioned IOPS / API named io1. Configured for maximum IOPS for its size – 30 IOPS/GB, with a maximum of 20,000 IOPS
- **Silver**: EBS General Purpose SSD / API named gp2
- **Bronze**: EBS Magnetic / API named standard

We can check on the Flocker control node whether this volume was generated, with `flockerctl list`.

Deploying Spark, again

We choose a host where we want to run the Spark standalone manager, be `aws-105`, and tag it as such:

```
docker node update --label-add type=sparkmaster aws-105
```

Other nodes will host our Spark workers.

We start the Spark master on `aws-105`:

```
$ docker service create \
--container-label spark-master \
--network spark \
--constraint 'node.labels.type == sparkmaster' \
--publish 8080:8080 \
--publish 7077:7077 \
--publish 6066:6066 \
--name spark-master \
--replicas 1 \
--env SPARK_MASTER_IP=0.0.0.0 \
--mount type=volume,target=/data,source=spark,volume-driver=flocker \
fsoppelsa/spark-master
```

First, the image. I discovered that there are some annoying things included into the Google images (such as unsetting some environment variables, so making a configuration from external, with --env switches, impossible). Thus, I created myself a pair of Spark 1.6.2 master and worker images.

Then, `--network`. Here we say to this container to attach to the user-defined overlay network called spark.

Finally, storage: `--mount`, which works with Docker volumes. We specify it to:

- Work with a volume: `type=volume`
- Mount the volume inside the container on `/data`: `target=/data`
- Use the `spark` volume that we created previously: `source=spark`
- Use Flocker as a `volume-driver`

When you create a service and mount a certain volume, if volume does not exist, it will get created.

 The current releases of Flocker only support replicas of 1. The reason being that iSCSI/block level mounts cannot be attached across multiple nodes. So only one service can use a volume at a given point of time with replica factor of 1. This makes Flocker more useful for storing and moving database data (which is what it's used for, especially). But here we'll use it to show a tiny example with persistent data in `/data` in the Spark master container.

So, with this configuration, let's add the workhorses, three Spark workers:

```
$ docker service create \
--constraint 'node.labels.type != sparkmaster' \
--network spark \
--name spark-worker \
--replicas 3 \
--env SPARK\_MASTER\_IP=10.0.0.3 \
--env SPARK\_WORKER\_CORES=1 \
--env SPARK\_WORKER\_MEMORY=1g \
fsoppelsa/spark-worker
```

Here, we pass some environment variables into the container, to limit resources usage to 1 core and 1G of memory per container.

After some minutes, this system is up, we connect to `aws-105`, port `8080` and see this page:

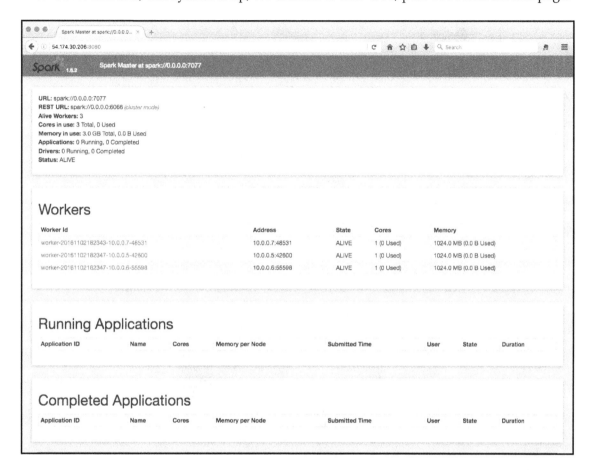

Testing Spark

So, we access the Spark shell and run a Spark task to check if things are up and running.

We prepare a container with some Spark utilities, for example, `fsoppelsa/spark-worker`, and run it to compute the value of Pi using the Spark binary `run-example`:

```
docker run -ti fsoppelsa/spark-worker /spark/bin/run-example
SparkPi
```

After a ton of output messages, Spark finishes the computation giving us:

```
...
Pi is roughly 3.14916
...
```

If we go back to the Spark UI, we can see that our amazing Pi application was successfully completed.

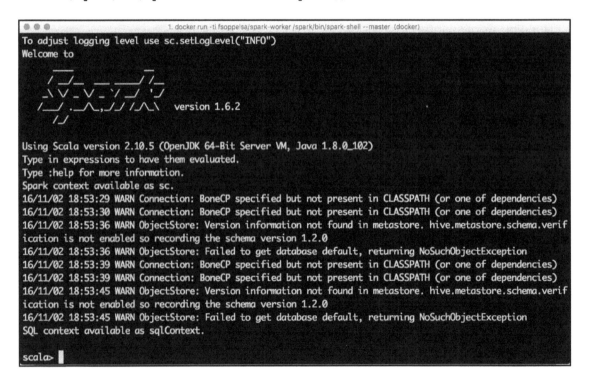

Completed Applications

Application ID	Name	Cores	Memory per Node	Submitted Time	User	State	Duration
app-20161102183712-0000	Spark shell	3	1024.0 MB	2016/11/02 18:37:12	root	FINISHED	12 min

More interesting is running an interactive Scala shell connecting to the master to execute Spark jobs:

```
$ docker run -ti fsoppelsa/spark-worker \
/spark/bin/spark-shell --master spark://<aws-105-IP>:7077
```

```
To adjust logging level use sc.setLogLevel("INFO")
Welcome to


      ____              __
     / __/__  ___ _____/ /__
    _\ \/ _ \/ _ `/ __/  '_/
   /___/ .__/\_,_/_/ /_/\_\   version 1.6.2
      /_/

Using Scala version 2.10.5 (OpenJDK 64-Bit Server VM, Java 1.8.0_102)
Type in expressions to have them evaluated.
Type :help for more information.
Spark context available as sc.
16/11/02 18:53:29 WARN Connection: BoneCP specified but not present in CLASSPATH (or one of dependencies)
16/11/02 18:53:30 WARN Connection: BoneCP specified but not present in CLASSPATH (or one of dependencies)
16/11/02 18:53:36 WARN ObjectStore: Version information not found in metastore. hive.metastore.schema.verif
ication is not enabled so recording the schema version 1.2.0
16/11/02 18:53:36 WARN ObjectStore: Failed to get database default, returning NoSuchObjectException
16/11/02 18:53:39 WARN Connection: BoneCP specified but not present in CLASSPATH (or one of dependencies)
16/11/02 18:53:39 WARN Connection: BoneCP specified but not present in CLASSPATH (or one of dependencies)
16/11/02 18:53:45 WARN ObjectStore: Version information not found in metastore. hive.metastore.schema.verif
ication is not enabled so recording the schema version 1.2.0
16/11/02 18:53:45 WARN ObjectStore: Failed to get database default, returning NoSuchObjectException
SQL context available as sqlContext.

scala>
```

Using Flocker storage

Only for the purpose of this tutorial, we now run an example using the spark volume we created previously to read and write some persistent data from Spark.

In order to do that and because of Flocker limitation of the replica factor, we kill the current set of three workers and create a set of only one, mounting spark:

```
$ docker service rm spark-worker
$ docker service create \
--constraint 'node.labels.type == sparkmaster' \
--network spark \
--name spark-worker \
--replicas 1 \
--env SPARK\_MASTER\_IP=10.0.0.3 \
--mount type=volume,target=/data,source=spark,volume-driver=flocker\
fsoppelsa/spark-worker
```

We now gain the Docker credentials of host `aws-105` with:

```
$ eval $(docker-machine env aws-105)
```

We can try to write some data in /data by connecting to the Spark master container. In this example, we just save some text data (The content of lorem ipsum, available for example at http://www.loremipsum.net) to /data/file.txt.

```
$ docker exec -ti 13ad1e671c8d bash
# echo "the content of lorem ipsum" > /data/file.txt
```

Then, we connect to the Spark shell to execute a simple Spark job:

1. Load `file.txt`.
2. Map the words it contains to the number of their occurrences.
3. Save the result in `/data/output`:

```
$ docker exec -ti 13ad1e671c8d /spark/bin/spark-shell
...
scala> val inFile = sc.textFile("file:/data/file.txt")
scala> val counts = inFile.flatMap(line => line.split("
")).map(word => (word, 1)).reduceByKey(_ + _)
scala> counts.saveAsTextFile("file:/data/output")
scala> ^D
```

```
scala> val inFile = sc.textFile("file:/data/file.txt")
inFile: org.apache.spark.rdd.RDD[String] = file:/data/file.txt MapPartitionsRDD[1] at textFile at <console>:27

scala> val counts = inFile.flatMap(line => line.split(" ")).map(word => (word, 1)).reduceByKey(_ + _)
counts: org.apache.spark.rdd.RDD[(String, Int)] = ShuffledRDD[4] at reduceByKey at <console>:29

scala> counts.saveAsTextFile("file:/data/output")

scala> Stopping spark context.
```

Now, let's start a `busybox` container on any Spark node and check the content of the `spark` volume, verifying that the output was written. We run the following code:

```
$ docker run -v spark:/data -ti busybox sh
# ls /data
# ls /data/output/
# cat /data/output/part-00000
```

```
➜ ~ docker run -v spark:/data -ti busybox sh
Unable to find image 'busybox:latest' locally
latest: Pulling from library/busybox
56bec22e3559: Pull complete
Digest: sha256:29f5d56d12684887bdfa50dcd29fc31eea4aaf4ad3bec43daf19026a7ce69912
Status: Downloaded newer image for busybox:latest
/ # ls /data
file.txt  output
/ # ls /data/output/
_SUCCESS    part-00000  part-00001
/ # cat /data/output/part-00000
(vulputate,1)
(interdum,1)
(ullamcorper,,1)
(porta,1)
(ac,3)
(neque,1)
(lacus.,1)
(ante,1)
```

The preceding screenshot shows the output, as expected. The interesting thing about Flocker volume is that they can be even moved from one host to another. A number of operations can be done in a reliable way. Flocker is a good idea if one is looking for a good storage solution for Docker. For example, it's used in production by the Swisscom Developer cloud (http://developer.swisscom.com/), which lets you provision databases such as **MongoDB** backed by Flocker technology. Upcoming releases of Flocker will aim at slimming down the Flocker codebase and making it more lean and durable. Items such as built in HA, snapshotting, certificate distribution, and easily deployable agents in containers are some of things that are up next. So, a bright future!

Scaling Spark

Now we illustrate the most amazing feature of Swarm Mode–the `scale` command. We restore the configuration we had before trying Flocker, so we destroy the `spark-worker` service and re-create it with a replica factor of 3:

```
aws-101$ docker service create \
--constraint 'node.labels.type != sparkmaster' \
--network spark \
--name spark-worker \
--replicas 3 \
--env SPARK_MASTER_IP=10.0.0.3 \
--env SPARK\_WORKER\_CORES=1 \
--env SPARK\_WORKER\_MEMORY=1g \
fsoppelsa/spark-worker
```

Now, we scale up the service with 30 Spark workers using the following code:

```
aws-101$ docker service scale spark-worker=30
```

After some minutes, necessary to eventually pull the image, we check once again:

From the Spark web UI:

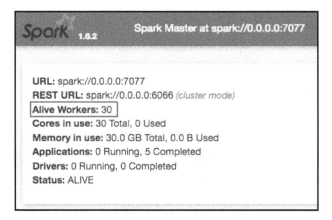

Scale can be used to scale up or down the size of the replicas. So far, still there are no automated mechanisms for auto-scaling or for distributing the load to newly added nodes. But they can be implemented with custom utilities, or we may even expect them to be integrated into Swarm soon day.

Monitoring Swarm hosting apps

I (Fabrizio) was following a thread on Reddit (https://www.reddit.com/r/docker/comments/4zous1/monitoring_containers_under_11 2_swarm/) in August 2016, where users complained that the new Swarm Mode is harder to monitor.

If, for now, there are no official Swarm monitoring solutions, one of the most popular combinations of emerging technologies is: Google's **cAdvisor** to collect data, **Grafana** to show graphs, and **Prometheus** as the data model.

Prometheus

The team at Prometheus describes the product as:

> *Prometheus is an open-source systems monitoring and alerting toolkit originally built at SoundCloud.*

Prometheus's main features are:

- Multi-dimensional data model
- A flexible query language
- No reliance on distributed storage
- Time series collection happens via a pull model
- Pushing time series is supported via a gateway
- Multiple modes of graphing and dashboarding support

There is a great presentation on `https://prometheus.io/docs/introduction/overview/` that we will not repeat here. The top feature of Prometheus is, in our opinion, the ease of installation and usage. Prometheus itself consists of just a single binary built from Go code, plus a configuration file.

Installing a monitoring system

Things are probably going to change very soon, so we just sketch a way to set up a monitoring system for Swarm, tried on Docker version 1.12.3.

First, we create a new overlay network to not interfere with the `ingress` or `spark` networks, called `monitoring`:

```
aws-101$ docker network create --driver overlay monitoring
```

Then, we start a cAdvisor service in mode `global`, meaning that a cAdvisor container will run on each Swarm node. We mount some system paths inside the container so that they can be accessed by cAdvisor:

```
aws-101$ docker service create \
  --mode global \
  --name cadvisor \
  --network monitoring \
  --mount type=bind,src=/var/lib/docker/,dst=/var/lib/docker \
  --mount type=bind,src=/,dst=/rootfs \
  --mount type=bind,src=/var/run,dst=/var/run \
  --publish 8080 \
  google/cadvisor
```

Then we use `basi/prometheus-swarm` to set up Prometheus:

```
aws-101$ docker service create \
  --name prometheus \
  --network monitoring \
  --replicas 1 \
  --publish 9090:9090 \
  prom/prometheus-swarm
```

And we add the `node-exporter` service (again `global`, must run on each node):

```
aws-101$ docker service create \
  --mode global \
  --name node-exporter \
  --network monitoring \
  --publish 9100 \
  prom/node-exporter
```

Finally, we start **Grafana** with one replica:

```
aws-101$ docker service create \
  --name grafana \
  --network monitoring \
  --publish 3000:3000 \
  --replicas 1 \
  -e "GF_SECURITY_ADMIN_PASSWORD=password" \
  -e "PROMETHEUS_ENDPOINT=http://prometheus:9090" \
  grafana/grafana
```

Importing Prometheus in Grafana

When Grafana is available, to get impressive graphs of the Swarm health, we login with these credentials on the node where Grafana runs, port 3000:

```
"admin":"password"
```

As admins, we click on the Grafana logo, go to**Data Sources**, and add Prometheus:

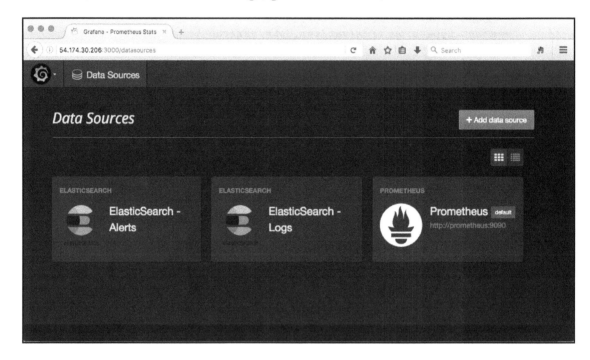

Some options will appear, but the mapping is already present, so it's sufficient to **Save & Test**:

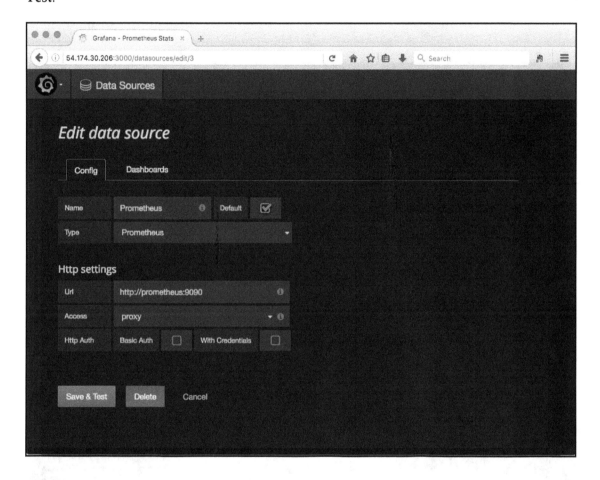

Now we can go back to the Dashboard and click on **Prometheus**, so we will be presented the Grafana main panel:

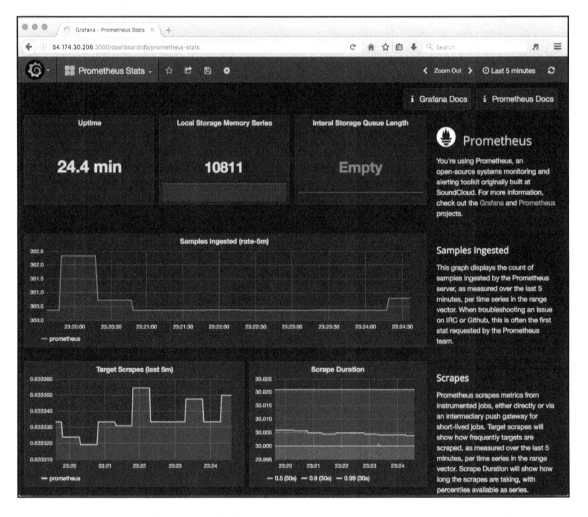

Once again, we took advantage of what the open source community released, and glued different opinionated technologies with just some simple commands, to get the desired result. Monitoring Docker Swarm and its applications is a field of research that is completely open now, so we can expect an amazing evolution there too.

Summary

In this chapter, we added storage capacity to a Swarm infrastructure using Flocker, and set a dedicated overlay network to make our example app, a Spark cluster, to work on it and be easily extendible by adding new nodes (also on new providers, such as DigitalOcean). After using our Spark installation and Flocker, we finally introduced Prometheus and Grafana to monitor the Swarm health and status. We will see new additional features that can be plugged into Swarm and how to secure a Swarm infrastructure in the next two chapters.

8
Exploring Additional Features of Swarm

In this chapter, we're going to discuss and deepen our knowledge on two very important topics related to Docker and orchestration systems: networking and consensus. In particular, we'll see how to:

- Foundations of Libnetwork
- Basic security of Libnetwork
- Routing mesh
- Overlay networks
- The Network Control Plane
- Libkv

Libnetwork

Libnetwork is the networking stack designed from the ground-up to work with Docker regardless of platforms, environments, operating systems, or infrastructures. Libnetwork is not only an interface for the network driver. It's not only a library to manage VLAN or VXLAN networks but it does more.

Libnetwork is a full networking stack and consists of three planes, the **Management Plane**, the **Control Plane**, and the **Data Plane** as shown in the following diagram:

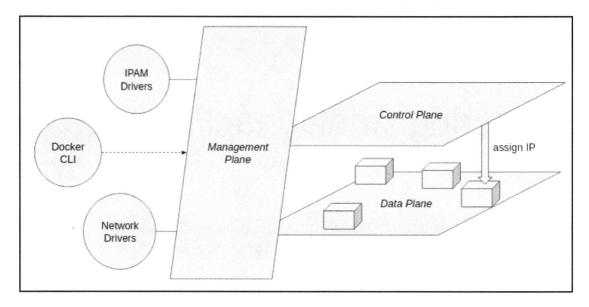

- The **Management Plane** allows users, operators, or tools to manage the network infrastructure. These operations include network monitoring. The Management Plane represents the Docker network user experiences, provides the APIs. It's also extensible via management plugins, such as IPAM plugins, which, for example, allows us to control how we assign IP addresses to each container.
- The **Control Plane** is implemented in the -scoped gossip protocol, service-discovery, encryption key distribution is added directly.
- In brief, the **Data Plane** is responsible for moving network packets between two Endpoints. Network plugins work for each Data Plane. By default, there are a few built-in drivers. For example, the overlay driver we met in the previous chapters directly uses the features inside Linux and Windows kernels, so there is no driver code for this kind of network. This is also applied for bridge, IPVLAN, and MacVLAN drivers. In contrast, other third-party networks need their own implementation in the form of plugins.

Following the usual Docker UX, that states the components should just work on any environment, also the networking stack must be portable. And to make Docker's networking stack portable, its design and implementation must be solid. For example, the Management Plane cannot be controlled by any other component. Also, the Control Plane cannot be replaced by other components. If we allowed that, the networking stack would break when we change our application environment from one to another.

Networking plugins

The Data Plane is designed to be pluggable. In fact, it can be only managed by built-in or external plugins. For example, MacVLAN was implemented as a plugin into Docker 1.12 without affecting other parts of the system.

The most remarkable thing is that we can have several Drivers and plugins on the same networking stack they can work without interfering with one another. So typically, in Swarm, we can have an overlay network, a bridge network as well as a host driver running on the same cluster.

Container Networking Model

Libnetwork is designed and implemented to serve the Docker Swarm requirements to run Docker's distributed applications. That is, Libnetwork is actually the Docker Networking Fabric. The foundation of Libnetwork is a model called **Container Networking Model (CNM)**. It is a well-defined basic model that describes how containers connect to the given networks. The CNM consists of three components:

- **Sandbox**: This is an isolation containing the configuration of the network stack of the container.
- **Endpoint**: This is a connection point that only belongs to a network and a sandbox.
- **Network**: This is a group of endpoints which allowed to community freely among them. A network consists of one or more endpoints.

The Drivers represent the Data Plane. Every Driver, being overlay, bridge, or MacVLAN are in the form of Plugins. Each plugin works in a Data Plane specific to it.

In the system, there is a built-in IPAM by default. This is an important issue because each container must have an IP address attached. So it's necessary to have an IPAM system built-in, which allows each container to be able to connect to each otheras we did in the traditional way and we need an IP address for others to talk to the container. We also require to define subnets as well as ranges of IP addresses. Also, the system is designed for IPAM to be pluggable. This means that it allows us to have our own DHCP drivers or allow plumbing the system to an existing DHCP server.

As previously mentioned, Libnetwork supports multihost networking out-of-the-box. Components worth to discuss for the multihost networking are its Data and Control Planes.

The Control Plane currently included in Docker 1.12 uses the gossip mechanism as the general discovery system for nodes. This gossip protocol-based network works on another layer in parallel of the Raft consensus system. Basically, we have twodifferent membership mechanisms work at the same time. Libnetwork allows the driver from other plugins to commonly use the control plane.

These are the features of Libnetwork's Control plane:

- It's secure and encrypted out-of-the-box
- Every single data plane can use it
- It provides native service discovery and load balancing out-of-the-box

Docker 1.12 implements VIP-based service discovery in Swarm. This service works by mapping a Virtual IP address of the container to the DNS records. Then all DNS records are shared via gossip. In Docker 1.12, with the introduction of the concept of service, this notion fits directly to the concept of discovery.

In Docker 1.11 and previous versions, it was necessary instead to use container names and aliases to "simulate" service discovery and do DNS roundrobin to perform some kind of primitive load balancing.

Libnetwork carries on the principle of battery included but removable, which is implemented as the plugin system. In the future, Libnetwork will gradually expand the plugin system to cover other networking parts, for example, load balancing.

Encryption and routing mesh

The model at the heart of Libnetwork is CNM, as previously mentioned. In Swarm mode, libnetwork is built in a cluster-aware mode and supports multi-host networking without external key value stores. The overlay network fits naturally in this model. And both Data plane and Control plane encryption has been introduced. With encrypted Control Plane, routing information on VXLAN, for example, for which container has which MAC address and which IP address, is automatically secured. Also, with Routing Mesh, CNM provides a decentralized mechanism allowing you to access services from any IP of the cluster. When a request comes from the outsideand hits any node of the cluster, the traffic will be routed to a working container.

MacVLAN

The new Driver in 1.12 is MacVLAN. MacVLAN is a performant driver designed to allow the Docker network to plumb to the existing VLAN, for example, a corporate one, letting everything to continue to work. There is a scenario where we will gradually migrate workloads from the original VLAN to Docker and MacVLAN will help plumb the Docker cluster to the original VLAN. This will make the Docker networks integrated with the underlay network and the containers will be able to work in the same VLAN.

We could just create a network with the MacVLAN driver and specify the real subnet to the network. We can also specify a range of IP addresses only for the containers. Also, we can exclude some IP addresses, for example, the gateway, from assigning to containers with `--aux-address`. The parent interface of the MacVLAN driver is the interface we would like to connect this network to. As previously mentioned, MacVLAN yields the best performance of all drivers. Its Linux implementation isextremely lightweight. They just enforce the separation between networks and connection to the physical parent network, rather than implemented as traditional Linux bridge for network isolation. The use of MacVLAN driver requires Linux Kernel 3.9 – 3.19 or 4.x.

Overlay networks

Because Swarm cluster is now a native feature built into the Docker Engine, this allows the creation of overlay networks very easy without using external key-value stores.

Manager nodes are responsible for managing the state of the networks. All the networking states are kept inside the Raft log. The main difference between Raft implementation in the Swarm mode and the external key-value store is that the embedded Raft has far higher performance than the external ones. Our own experiments confirmed that the external key-value store will stick around 100-250 nodes, while the embedded Raft helped us scale the system to 4,700 nodes in the Swarm3k event. This is because the external Raft store basically has high network latency. When we need to agree on some states, we will be incurred from the network round-trips, while the embedded Raft store is just there in memory.

In the past, when we wanted to do any network-related action, assigning IP address to the containers, for example, significant network latency happened as we always talk to the external store. For the embedded Raft, when we would like to have a consensus on values, we can do it right away with the in-memory store.

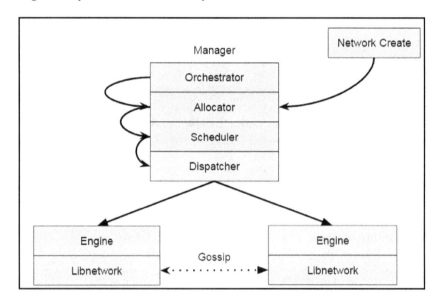

When we create a network with the overlay driver, as follows:

```
$ docker network create --driver overlay --subnet 10.9.0.0/24 mh_net
```

The command will talk to the allocator. Then there will be a subnet reservation, in this case `10.9.0.0/24`, and agree related values right away in the manager host in its memory once it's allocated. We would like to create a service after that. Then we will later connect that service to the network. When we create a service, as follows:

```
$ docker service create --network mh_net nginx
```

The orchestrator creates a number of tasks (containers) for that service. Then each created task will be assigned an IP address. The allocation will be working again during this assignment.

After the task creation is done:

- The task gets an IP address
- Its network-related information will be committed into the Raft log store
- After the commit is done by the allocation, the scheduler will be moving the task to another state
- The Dispatcher dispatches each task to one of the worker nodes
- Finally, the container associated to that task will be running on the Docker Engine

If a task is not able to allocate its network resource, it will be stuck there at the allocated state and will not be scheduled. This is the important difference from the previous versions of Docker that in the network system of Swarm mode, the concept of allocation state is obvious. With this, it improves the overall allocation cycle of the system a lot. When we talk about the allocation, we refer not only to the allocation of IP addresses, but also to related driver artifacts. For an overlay network, it needs to reserve a VXLAN identifier, which is a set of global identifiers for each VXLAN. This identifier reservation is done by the Network Allocator.

In the future, for a plugin to do the same allocation mechanism, it will be enough to implement only some interfaces and make the state being automatically managed by Libnetwork and stored into the Raft log. With this, the resource allocation is in the centralized way, so we can achieve consistency and consensus. With consensus, we need a highly efficient consensus protocol.

Network Control Plane

Network Control Plane is a subsystem of Libnetwork to manage routing information and we need a protocol that converge quickly to do that job. For example, Libnetwork does not use BGP as the protocol (despite that BGP is great at scalability to support very large number of endpoints), because point BGP won't converge quick enough to use in the highly dynamic environment such as the software container environment.

In a container-centric world, the networking system is expected to change very quickly, especially for the new Docker service model, which requires a massive and fast IP assignation. We want the routing information to converge very rapidly as well, especially at a big scale, for example, for more than 10,000 containers. In Swarm2k and Swarm3k experiments, we really did start 10,000 containers at a time. Especially, in Swarm3k, we started 4,000 NGINX containers on the Ingress load-balancing network. Without a fine implementation, this number of scale won't work correctly.

To solve this problem, the Libnetwork team chose to include the gossip protocol in the Network Control Plane. The internal algorithm of the protocol works like this: It choses 3 neighbors and then propagates the same information; in the case of Libnetwork, the routing and other network related information. The Gossip protocol will do this process repeatedly, until every node shares the same information. With this technique, the whole cluster will receive the information very quickly, in a matter of seconds.

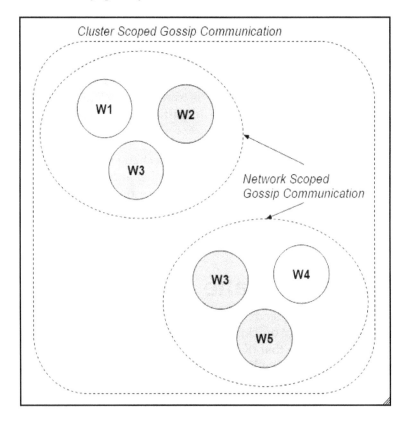

Anyway, the whole cluster does not need the same information all the time. Every node on the cluster does not need to know information of all the networks. Only nodes in a particular network need to know its own networking information. To optimize this for Libnetwork, the team implemented two scopes, *Cluster Scoped Gossip Communication* and *Network Scoped Gossip Communication*. What we have explained so far is the Cluster Scope Gossip Communication, while Network Scoped Gossip Communication limits the network information within a particular network. When a network expands to cover addition nodes, its gossip scoped broadcast will also cover them.

This activity is built on top Docker's CNM and therefore relieson the network abstraction. From the Figure, we have node **w1**, **w2**, and **w3** in the Left network and also **w3**, **w4**, **w5** in the right network. The left network performs gossip and only **w1**, **w2**, **w3** would know its routing information. You may observe that w3 is in both the networks. Therefore, it will receive routing information of all left and right networks.

Libkv

libkv is a unified library to interact with different key-value store backends. libkv was originally part of Docker Swarm v1 in the very first versions of the development. Later, all code related to key-value store discovery services was refactored and moved to www.github.com/docker/libkv.

`libkv` allows you to execute CRUD operations and also to watch key-value entries from different backends, so we can use the same code to work with all HA distributed key-value stores, which are **Consul**, **Etcd**, and **ZooKeeper** as shown in the following figure. At the time of writing, libkv also supports a local store implemented using **BoltDB**.

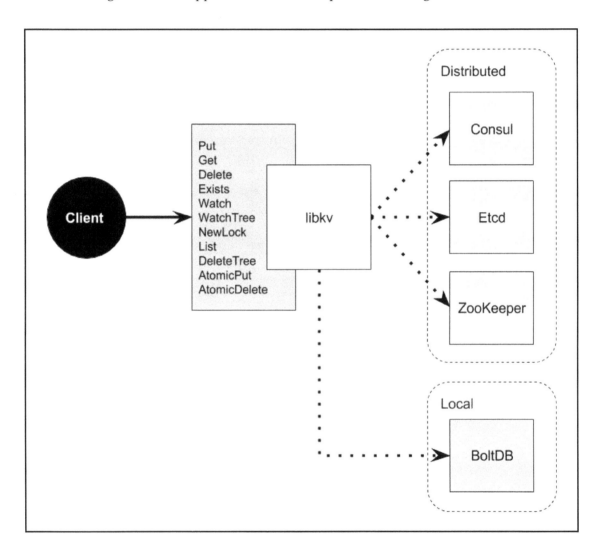

How to use libkv

To start with `libkv`, we need to understand how to call its APIs first. Here's the `libkv` `Store` interface in Go, for every store implementation:

```go
type Store interface {
    Put(key string, value []byte, options *WriteOptions) error
    Get(key string) (*KVPair, error)
    Delete(key string) error
    Exists(key string) (bool, error)
    Watch(key string, stopCh <-chan struct{}) (<-chan *KVPair, error)
    WatchTree(directory string, stopCh <-chan struct{}) (<-chan
    []*KVPair,
    error)
    NewLock(key string, options *LockOptions) (Locker, error)
    List(directory string) ([]*KVPair, error)
    DeleteTree(directory string) error
    AtomicPut(key string, value []byte, previous *KVPair, options
    *WriteOptions) (bool, *KVPair, error)
    AtomicDelete(key string, previous *KVPair) (bool, error)
    Close()
}
```

We need to know how to `Put`, `Get`, `Delete`, and `Watch` to basically interact with a store.

Make sure you also have Go and Git installed on your machine and the Git executable is on your PATH. Then, we need to do a number of go get to install dependencies for our program:

```
$ go get github.com/docker/libkv
$ go get github.com/davecgh/go-spew/spew
$ go get github.com/hashicorp/consul/api
```

Here we provide with a skeleton. You need to start a single-node `Consul` before you try to run the following program:

```
# Delete all keys in Consul
$ curl -X DELETE http://localhost:8500/v1/kv/?recurse
# Compile the program
$ go build main.go
# Run it
$ ./main
# Spew is dumping the result for us in details
([]*store.KVPair) (len=1 cap=2) {
(*store.KVPair)(0x10e00de0)({
 Key: (string) (len=27) "docker/nodes/127.0.0.1:2375",
 Value: ([]uint8) (len=14 cap=15) {
```

```
00000000   31 32 37 2e 30 2e 30 2e   31 3a 32 33 37 35
|127.0.0.1:2375|
},
LastIndex: (uint64) 736745
})
}
```

You can also test getting your value with curl. The value you've put should be there. We should continue playing with the libkv APIs,which are `Get` and `Delete`. It's left for the readers as an exercise.

Summary

This chapter covers Libnetwork, one of the most important parts of Docker Swarm. We have discussed its Management Plane, Control Plane, and Data Plane. This chapter also includes some techniques on how to use `libkv`, a key-value abstraction to implement your own service discovery system. In the next chapter, we'll focus on security. In the next chapter, we will learn how to secure a swarm cluster.

9

Securing a Swarm Cluster and the Docker Software Supply Chain

This chapter is all about Swarm cluster security. In particular, we'll take a look at the following topics:

- The Software supply chain with Docker
- Recommendations on how to secure a Swarm cluster
- Use Docker Notary to secure the Software supply chain

Software Supply Chain

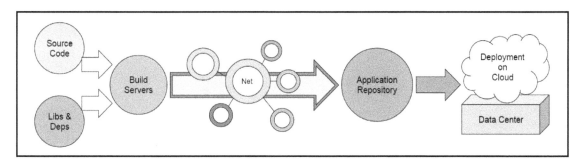

Docker orchestration is only a component of the larger software supply chain. We basically start with *Source Code* as the raw material. Our source code is compiled and linked with *Library and Dependent packages*. We use *Build Service* to continuously integrate our Source Code and its Dependencies together and finally assemble them as a *Product*. We then ship the Product on the Internet, to store it somewhere else. We usually call this warehouse an *Application Repository* or simply a *repository*. Finally, we send the product to the customer's environment, for example a cloud or a physical data center.

Docker is perfect for this workflow. Developers use Docker locally to compile and test applications, system administrators deploy these applications on the Build Servers using Docker, and Docker may also play an important role in the process of continuous integration.

Security kicks in here. We need a secure way to sign our products before pushing it to the Application Repository. In our Docker-centric world, we store ready products in a warehouse called *Docker Registry*. Then a signed product will be verified, each time, before it is deployed to the production system where we're running our Docker Swarm mode cluster.

In the remainder of the chapter, we will talk about the following two aspects of security:

- How to secure a production Swarm cluster, which we achieve with best practices
- How to secure the software supply chain, which we achieve with Docker Notary

Securing Swarm cluster

Recall the picture of a secured Swarm cluster from `Chapter 4`, *Creating a Production-Grade Swarm*; we'll explain the security aspects found in a Docker Swarm model cluster.

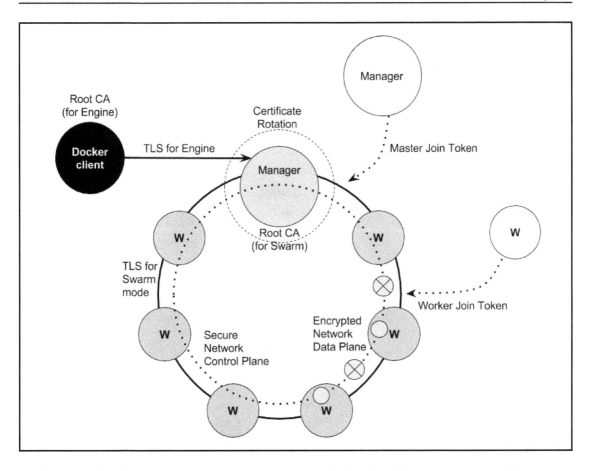

We have the Orchestrator as one of the main parts of a Docker Swarm manager. Diogo Monica, a member of the Docker Security team, mentioned in his Orchestration Least Privileged presentation, in Berlin 2016, that each component in the orchestration must have a limitation of what it can do.

- **Node management**: A cluster operator may instruct an Orchestrator to perform actions for a set of nodes
- **Task assignment**: The Orchestrator is also responsible for assigning tasks to each node

- **Cluster state reconciliation**: The Orchestrator maintains the state of the cluster by reconciling each state to the desired state
- **Resource management**: The Orchestrator offers and revokes resources for submitted tasks

An Orchestrator with the least privilege will make the system secure and a least privilege Orchestrator is defined based on these functionalities. Following the principle of least privilege, a manager as well as the workers must be able to access *only the information and resource that are necessary to perform a given task.*

Also, Diogo presented the following list of five different attacking models that can be applied to Docker. They are listed from the lowest to the highest risk.

- **External attacker**: Outside of the firewall trying to compromise the cluster.
- **Internal attacker**: Doesn't own the switch but has access to the switch. It can send packets to communicate with nodes in the cluster.
- **Man-in-the-middle**: An attacker who can listen to everything going in the network and can conduct an active attack. With this model, there is a Swarm cluster and the communications of worker nodes to the manager nodes are intercepted.
- **Malicious worker node**: The resources owned by the worker are effectively owned by the attacker.
- **Malicious manager node**: The manager is an attacker who can control the complete Orchestrator and gain access to all available resources. It is the worst case scenario. If we could implement the least privileges, the malicious manager node can only attack the workers associated to it.

Securing a Swarm: Best practices

We will now summarize the checklist for securing a Swarm cluster. The Swarm team is working hard to achieve the goals of preventing attacks on the full stack, but the following rules apply in any case.

Certification Authorities

The first important step to guarantee security is deciding on how to use CA. When you form a cluster with the first node, it will automatically create a self-signed CA for the whole cluster. After spinning up, it creates CA, signs the certificate itself, adds the certificate for the manager, which is itself, and becomes the ready-to-operate 1-node cluster. When a new node joins, it gets the certificate by providing the correct token. Every node has its own identity which is cryptographically signed. Also, the system has a certificate for each rule, worker, or manager. The role is inside the identity information to tell who a node is. In the case that a manager leaks the root CA, the whole cluster is compromised. Docker Swarm mode supports external CAs to maintain the manager's identity. The manager can simply forward the CSR to the external CA so it does not need to maintain its own CA. Please note that the only protocol supported at this moment is `cfssl`. The following command is to init the cluster with the external CA.

```
$ docker swarm init --external-ca \
protocol=cfssl,url=https://ca.example.com
```

Certificates and Mutual TLS

Every single endpoint communication on the network control plane must have a mutual TLS and is encrypted and authorized by default. This means that a worker cannot fake to be a manager and no external attacker can connect to an endpoint and successfully complete the TLS handshake because the attacker does not have the keys to mutually authenticate itself. This means that each node must provide a valid CA-signed certificate, which has the OU field that matches each rule of the cluster. If a worker connects to the manager endpoint, it will be denied access.

The Certificate rotation is done automatically by Swarm. You can have the certificate rotation as short as one hour in SwarmKit and also Docker Swarm mode. The following is the command to adjust the certificate expiry time.

```
$ docker swarm update --cert-expiry 1h
```

The join token

Each token, used by nodes to join the cluster, has the following four components:

- SWMTKN, the Swarm prefix that allows finding, or grepping, when tokens are leaked
- The token version, which is currently 1
- The cryptographically hashed value of the CA root certificate to allow bootstrap
- A randomly generated Secret

The following is an example of token:

```
SWMTKN-1-11lo1xx5bau6nmv5jox26rc5mr7l1mj5wi7b84w27v774frtko-
e82x3ti068m9eec9w7q2zp9fe
```

To access the cluster, it is necessary to send a token as proof. It is like the cluster password.

The good news is that in case of token compromising, the token can be *simply rotate*d using one of the following commands.

```
$ docker swarm join-token --rotate worker
$ docker swarm join-token --rotate manager
```

Add TLS with Docker Machine

Another good practice is provisioning all manager nodes with Docker Machine to set up an extra layer of TLS, automatically, so that each manager can be accessed by remote Docker clients in a secure manner. This can simply be done using the following command, similar to how we did in the previous chapter:

```
$ docker-machine create \
  --driver generic \
  --generic-ip-address=<IP> \
mg0
```

Form a cluster on a private network

If forming a hybrid cluster is not a requirement, one of the best practices is that we should form a cluster with all the nodes being on a local private network. With this, the data of overlay network will not need to be encrypted and the performance of cluster will be fast.

When forming this kind of cluster, the Routing Mesh allows us to expose any worker, not necessarily a manager, to the public-network interface. The following figure shows the cluster configuration. You can see that with this configuration and a Docker service published port 80 on the Ingress network. The routing mesh forms a star-like mesh but we simplified it and showed only one-side from the Big W node connecting IPVS load-balancing to others. The Big W node has two network interfaces. Its public interface allows the node to act as a front-end node of the whole cluster. With this architecture, we can achieve a certain level of security by not exposing any manager node to the public network.

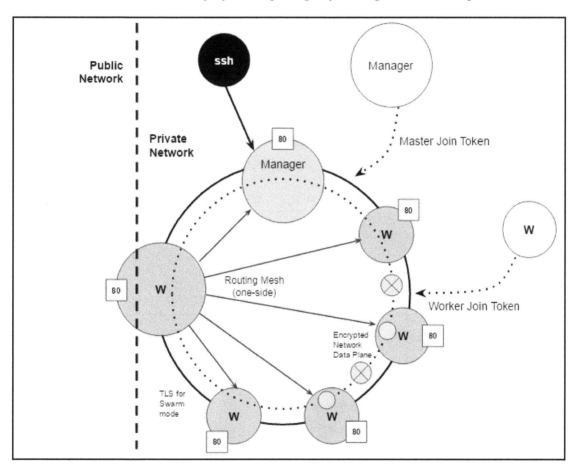

Docker Notary

The Docker Content Trust mechanism is implemented using Docker Notary (`https://gith ub.com/docker/notary`), which is on The Update Framework (`https://github.com/theupdateframework/tuf`). TUF is a secure framework that allows us to delivery a collection of trusted content at a time. Notary allows a client and a server to form a trusted *collection* by making it easier to publish and verify contents. If we have a Docker image, we can sign it offline using a highly secure offline key. Then when we publish that image, we can push it to a Notary server that can be used to delivery trusted images. Notary is the way to enable *Secured Software Supply Chain* for the enterprise using Docker.

We demonstrate how to set up our own Notary server and use it to sign Docker image content before pushing to a Docker registry. The prerequisite is to have a recent version of Docker Compose installed.

The first step is to clone Notary (in this example we fix its version at 0.4.2):

```
git clone https://github.com/docker/notary.git
cd notary
git checkout v0.4.2
cd notary
```

Open `docker-compose.yml` and add the image option to specify an image name and tag for both signer and server. In this example, I used Docker Hub to store the build images. So it's `chanwit/server:v042` and `chanwit/signer:v042`. Change this to reflect your local configuration.

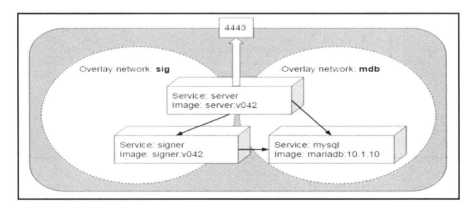

Then start with

```
$ docker-compose up -d
```

We now have a Notary server up and running at `https://127.0.0.1:4443`. To make it possible for the Docker client to do a handshake with Notary, we need to copy the Notary Server certificate as CA of this trusted address (`127.0.0.4443`).

```
$ mkdir -p ~/.docker/tls/127.0.0.1:4443/
$ cp ./fixtures/notary-server.crt
~/.docker/tls/127.0.0.1:4443/ca.crt
```

After that, we enable Docker Content Trust and point Docker Content Trust server to our own Notary at `https://127.0.0.1:4443`.

```
$ export DOCKER_CONTENT_TRUST=1
$ export DOCKER_CONTENT_TRUST_SERVER=https://127.0.0.1:4443
```

Then we tag the image as a new one and push the image while enabling Docker Content Trust:

```
$ docker tag busybox chanwit/busybox:signed
$ docker push chanwit/busybox:signed
```

If the setup finishes correctly, we'll see the Docker client asking for the new root key and the new repository key. Then it will confirm that `chanwit/busybox:signed` was successfully signed.

```
The push refers to a repository [docker.io/chanwit/busybox]
e88b3f82283b: Layer already exists
signed: digest:
sha256:29f5d56d12684887bdfa50dcd29fc31eea4aaf4ad3bec43daf19026a7ce69912
size: 527
Signing and pushing trust metadata
You are about to create a new root signing key passphrase. This
passphrase
will be used to protect the most sensitive key in your signing system.
Please
choose a long, complex passphrase and be careful to keep the password
and the
key file itself secure and backed up. It is highly recommended that you
use a
password manager to generate the passphrase and keep it safe. There
will be no
way to recover this key. You can find the key in your config directory.
Enter passphrase for new root key with ID 1bec0c1:
Repeat passphrase for new root key with ID 1bec0c1:
```

```
    Enter passphrase for new repository key with ID ee73739
(docker.io/chanwit/busybox):
    Repeat passphrase for new repository key with ID ee73739
(docker.io/chanwit/busybox):
    Finished initializing "docker.io/chanwit/busybox"
    Successfully signed "docker.io/chanwit/busybox":signed
```

Now, we can try pulling the same image:

```
$ docker pull chanwit/busybox:signed
    Pull (1 of 1):
chanwit/busybox:signed@sha256:29f5d56d12684887bdfa50dcd29fc31eea4aaf4ad3bec
43daf19026a7ce69912
sha256:29f5d56d12684887bdfa50dcd29fc31eea4aaf4ad3bec43daf19026a7ce69912:
Pulling from chanwit/busybox
    Digest:
sha256:29f5d56d12684887bdfa50dcd29fc31eea4aaf4ad3bec43daf19026a7ce69912
    Status: Image is up to date for
chanwit/busybox@sha256:29f5d56d12684887bdfa50dcd29fc31eea4aaf4ad3bec43daf19
026a7ce69912
    Tagging
chanwit/busybox@sha256:29f5d56d12684887bdfa50dcd29fc31eea4aaf4ad3bec43daf19
026a7ce69912 as chanwit/busybox:signed
```

When we pull an unsigned image, and this time it will show that there is no trusted data:

```
$ docker pull busybox:latest
    Error: remote trust data does not exist for docker.io/library/busybox:
127.0.0.1:4443 does not have trust data for docker.io/library/busybox
```

Introducing Docker secrets

Docker 1.13 includes in Swarm the new concept of secrets management.

As we know, we need Swarm mode to use secrets. When we initialize a Swarm, Swarm generates some secrets for us:

```
$ docker swarm init
```

Docker 1.13 adds the secrets management with a new command, secret, with the purpose to handle them efficiently. Secret subcommands are created, ls, to inspect and rm.

Let's create our first secret. The `secret create` sub-command takes a secret from the standard input. So, we need to type in our secret, and then press *Ctrl+D* to save the content. Be careful to not hit the *Enter* key. We need only `1234` not `1234\n` as our password, for example:

```
$ docker secret create password
1234
```

Then press *Ctrl+D* twice to close the standard input.

We can check if there is a secret called password:

```
$ docker secret ls
ID                        NAME        CREATED          UPDATED
16blafexuvrv2hgznrjitj93s  password   25 seconds ago   25 seconds ago
uxep4enknneoevvqatstouec2  test-pass  18 minutes ago   18 minutes ago
```

How does this work? The content of secret can be bound to a service by passing the secret option when we create a new service. The secret will be a file in the `/run/secrets/` directory. In our case, we'll have `/run/secrets/password` containing the string `1234`.

Secrets are designed to replace the abuse of environment variables. For example, in the case of a MySQL or MariaDB container, its root password should be set as a secret instead of passing it as a plaintext via an environment variable.

We will show a small hack to make MariaDB support the new Swarm secrets, starting from the following `entrypoint.sh`:

```
$ wget https://raw.githubusercontent.com/docker-
library/mariadb/2538af1bad7f05ac2c23dc6eb35e8cba6356fc43/10.1/docker-
entrypoint.sh
```

We put this line into this script, around line 56, before the check of `MYSQL_ROOT_PASSWORD`.

```
    # check secret file. if exist, override
    if [ -f "/run/secrets/mysql-root-password" ]; then
        MYSQL_ROOT_PASSWORD=$(cat /run/secrets/mysql-root-password)
    fi
```

This code checks if there exists `/run/secrets/mysql-root-password`. If so, it assigns the secret to the environment variable `MYSQL_ROOT_PASSWORD`.

After this we can prepare a Dockerfile to override the MariaDB's default `docker-entrypoint.sh`.

```
FROM mariadb:10.1.19
RUN  unlink /docker-entrypoint.sh
COPY docker-entrypoint.sh /usr/local/bin/
RUN  chmod +x /usr/local/bin/docker-entrypoint.sh
RUN  ln -s usr/local/bin/docker-entrypoint.sh /
```

We then build the new image.

```
$ docker build -t chanwit/mariadb:10.1.19 .
```

Recalled that we have a secret named password, we have an image which allows us to set the root password from the secret file `/run/secrets/mysql-root-password`. So, the image expects a different file name under `/run/secrets`. With this we can use the secret with full option (`source=password`, `target=mysql-root-password`) to make a Swarm service work. For example, we can now start a new `mysql` Swarm service from this MariaDB image:

```
$ docker network create -d overlay dbnet
1sc7prijmvg7sj6412b1jnsot
$ docker service create --name mysql \
   --secret source=password,target=mysql-root-password \
   --network dbnet \
   chanwit/mariadb:10.1.19
```

To see if our secret works, we can start an instance of PHPMyAdmin on the same overlay network. Don't forget to link these services together by passing `-e PMA_HOST=mysql` to the `myadmin` service.

```
$ docker service create --name myadmin \
   --network dbnet --publish 8080:80 \
   -e PMA_HOST=mysql \
   phpmyadmin/phpmyadmin
```

Then you can open your browser to `http://127.0.0.1:8080` and log in to PHPMyAdmin as root with `1234` as the password, which we provided through a Docker secret.

Summary

In this chapter, we learned about securing Swarm Mode and the Docker Software Supply Chain. We talked about some best practices on how to secure a Docker Swarm cluster to use in production. We then proceeded to Notary, a secure delivery mechanism to allow Docker Content Trust. This chapter ended with an overview of a new feature in Docker 1.13: the Secrets management. We showed how we could use Docker Secret to securely deploy MySQL MariaDB server without passing the root password via the environment. In the next chapter, we're going to discover how to deploy Swarm on some of the public cloud providers and on OpenStack.

10
Swarm and the Cloud

Throughout this book, we worked with Docker Swarm on a set of different underlying technologies without, so far, diving too deep into this implication: We ran Swarm on the top of AWS, DigitalOcean, and on our local workstations. For test and staging purposes, the platform onto which we run Swarm might be of secondary importance (*let's fire up some AWS instances with Docker Machine and work that way*), but for production it's mandatory to understand the pros and cons, reason, evaluate, and follow the trend.

In this chapter, we're going to review several public and private cloud options and technologies and their possible intersections. We'll finally treat the brand new buzzwords of **CaaS** (**Container as a Service**) and **IaaC** (**Infrastructure as a Code**) in `Chapter 11`, *What it Next?*

Mainly, we will be looking at:

- Docker for AWS and Azure
- Docker Datacenter
- Swarm on OpenStack

Docker for AWS and Azure

As long as with Docker For Mac and Windows, the Docker team started working on the *new generation* toolsets for operators: Docker for AWS and Docker for Windows. These are intended to provide a taste of automatic for deploying Docker infrastructures, especially Swarm-ready ones.

The goals are to provide with a standard way of doing things, integrating the underlying infrastructure with the Docker tools and let people to run, with no effort, the latest software versions on the platform they love. The ultimate goal is really to let developers to move things from their laptops with Docker for Mac/Windows to the cloud, with Docker for AWS/Azure.

Docker for AWS

The user experience is, as always in the Docker ecosystem, great. The requirements are:

- An AWS ID
- An SSH key imported into your AWS keyring
- Ready security groups

Basically, Docker for AWS is a clickable template for CloudForms. CloudForms is the orchestration system for AWS, which allows to create templates of complex systems, for example, you can specify a web infrastructure made of three web servers, one database, and one load balancer.

Instead of a web or other generic infrastructure, Docker for AWS of course comes with the capability of creating Docker Swarm (mode) infrastructures: it creates as many masters and workers as you specify, puts a load balancer in front, and configures all networking accordingly.

This is the welcome screen:

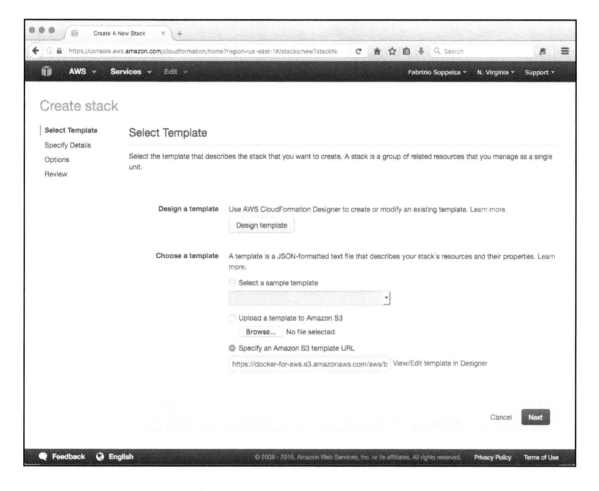

Then, you can specify some basic and advanced options:

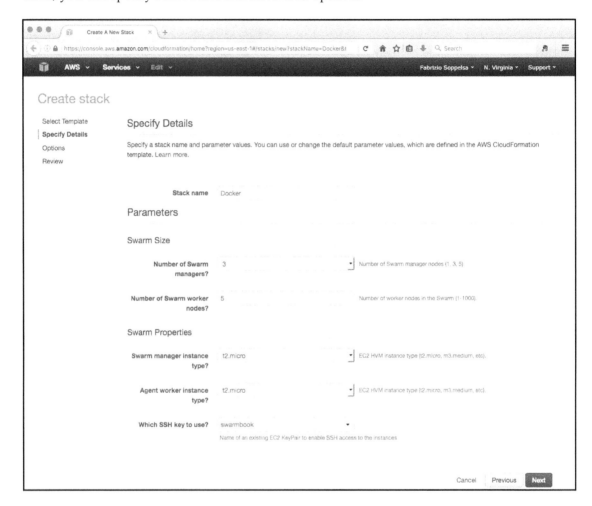

As you can see, you can select the number of managers and workers, as well as the flavor of the instances to be launched. So far, up to 1,000 workers are supported. After that, you just have to click on Create Stack in the next step, and wait for a few minutes for CloudForms to bring the infrastructure up.

What the template does is to:

1. Create a new Virtual Private Cloud inside your AWS account, networks, and subnets included.
2. Create two auto-scaling groups, One for managers and one for workers.
3. Start the managers and ensure that they are healthy up with Raft quorum reached.
4. Start and enroll the workers one by one to the Swarm.
5. Create **Elastic Load Balancers** (**ELBs**) to route traffic
6. Finish

Once CloudFormation has finished, it will prompt with a green confirmation.

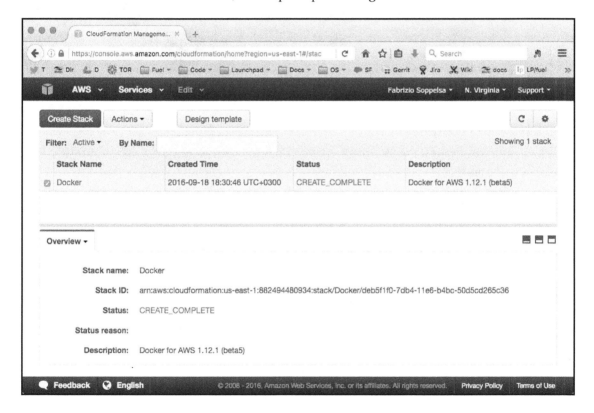

Now, we're ready to jump into our new Docker Swarm infrastructure. Just pick up one of the manager's public IPs and connect to it using the SSH key specified in the first step:

```
ssh docker@ec2-52-91-75-252.compute-1.amazonaws.com
```

```
●  ●  ●                    1. ssh docker@ec2-52-91-75-252.compute-1.amazonaws.com (ssh)
→  ~ ssh docker@ec2-52-91-75-252.compute-1.amazonaws.com
Welcome to Docker!
~ $ docker node ls
ID                          HOSTNAME                         STATUS   AVAILABILITY   MANAGER STATUS
27wl9f64nczoq2aoan6h47yzo   ip-192-168-34-247.ec2.internal   Ready    Active         Reachable
67ncghfxqsy38tdcyo7aja68x   ip-192-168-34-5.ec2.internal     Ready    Active
6u8pk9hm04aylwi9gjz071n0m   ip-192-168-33-174.ec2.internal   Ready    Active
6wqsm93ej4ecj59nv7ythlumh   ip-192-168-33-21.ec2.internal    Ready    Active         Reachable
8ffwsk9kqlwoyo89dmnnsc2d1   ip-192-168-34-4.ec2.internal     Ready    Active
a0mwx72m59vlnu15hx8es5nol   ip-192-168-33-173.ec2.internal   Ready    Active
cgh4aonn8aj0feqvrms1bxdi3 * ip-192-168-34-246.ec2.internal   Ready    Active         Leader
cximg853bqe473eym94b179ph   ip-192-168-33-175.ec2.internal   Ready    Active
~ $
```

Docker for Azure

Thanks to an agreement with Microsoft, also automatic Swarm deployment for Azure is available as a one-click experience (or almost).

The prerequisites for deploying Swarm on Azure are:

- Have a valid Azure account
- Have this account ID associated to Docker for Azure
- An Active Directory Principal application ID

To generate the last, you can conveniently use a docker image, and launch it with:

```
docker run -it docker4x/create-sp-azure docker-swarm
```

During the process, at some point, you will be required to login through a browser to the specified URL. At the end, a pair ID/secret will be available for you to input in the Azure wizard form.

```
● ● ●                    1. fsoppelsa@darthvader: ~ (zsh)
→  ~ docker run -it docker4x/create-sp-azure docker-swarm
info:      Executing command login
|info:     To sign in, use a web browser to open the page https://aka.ms/devi
celogin. Enter the code CBRTWWL4B to authenticate.
/
/info:     Added subscription Pay-As-You-Go
info:      Setting subscription "Pay-As-You-Go" as default
+
info:      login command OK
The following subscriptions were retrieved from your account
1) 08f28dc7-789a-472d-8afc-823be5bf9d16:Pay-As-You-Go
Please select the subscription to use: 1) 08f28dc7-789a-472d-8afc-823be5bf9d
16:Pay-As-You-Go
Please select the subscription to use: 1
Using subscription 08f28dc7-789a-472d-8afc-823be5bf9d16
Creating AD application docker-swarm
Created AD application, APP_ID=31076505-9b18-48ea-803d-6f2c97b28142
Creating AD App ServicePrincipal
Created ServicePrincipal ID=61a66b9a-fc1c-4f54-b669-9da819724ce2
Waiting for account updates to complete before proceeding.
Creating role assignment for 61a66b9a-fc1c-4f54-b669-9da819724ce2 for subscr
iption 08f28dc7-789a-472d-8afc-823be5bf9d16
Test login...


Your access credentials ═══════════════════════════════════════════════════
AD ServicePrincipal App ID:        31076505-9b18-48ea-803d-6f2c97b28142
AD ServicePrincipal App Secret:    1VK3nSGqH3YEeeNHegZYndlXhnzAFRvP
→  ~ █
```

Once everything is fine, you can just click on **OK** and **Create**.

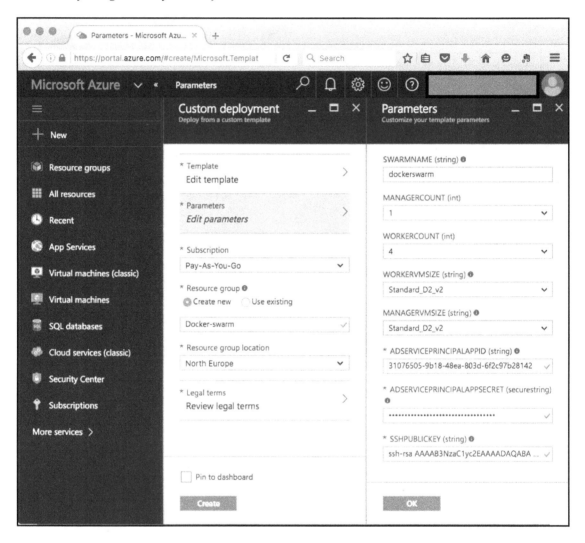

A set of classical virtual machines will be created to run the specified number of managers (here 1) and workers (here 4), as long as with the proper internal networks, load balancers, and routers. Just as in Docker for AWS, you can start using your deployed Swarm by SSHing to the public IP of one manager:

```
ssh docker@52.169.125.191
```

```
●  ●  ●                        1. ssh docker@52.169.125.191 (ssh)
→  ~ ssh docker@52.169.125.191
Welcome to Docker!
dockerswarm-manager0:~$ docker node ls
ID                            HOSTNAME                   STATUS  AVAILABILITY  MANAGER STATUS
25jfrlpwurckepsi5qirhk6ol *   _dockerswarm-manager0      Ready   Active        Leader
43wa4zt5j4vjz16md2h9k3qow     _dockerswarm-worker-vmss_2  Ready   Active
4jsosptkryiwjsy299txoxwv3     _dockerswarm-worker-vmss_1  Ready   Active
71w39o7mqvczky2eti6337vto     _dockerswarm-worker-vmss_0  Ready   Active
dockerswarm-manager0:~$ █
```

There is one limitation in the Azure template now, it only supports one manager. The possibility to add new managers should, however, come very soon.

Docker Datacenter

Docker Datacenter, formerly Tutum and acquired by Docker, is the single-click deploy solution by Docker to use UCP, the Universal Control Panel, Docker's commercial and enterprise product.

Docker Datacenter includes:

- **Universal Control Plane** (**UCP**), the UI, refer
  to https://docs.docker.com/ucp/overview
- **Docker Trusted Registry (DTR),** the private registry, refer to
  https://docs.docker.com/docker-trusted-registry

At the Dockercon 16, the team released support (currently in Beta) for Docker Datacenter running both on AWS and Azure. To try out Docker Datacenter, you need to associate a license to your company/project AWS or Azure ID.

For Datacenter for AWS, as for Docker for AWS, there is a CloudFormation template that makes immediate to start a Docker Datacenter. Requirements are:

- Have at least one Route53 configured, the AWS DNS service, see
  `http://docs.aws.amazon.com/Route53/latest/DeveloperGuide/Welcome.html`
- A Docker datacenter license

What you have to do is to follow the link from your license, to enter the Create Stack page. From here, you just input the **HostedZone** ID and the Docker Datacenter license and start the Stack creation. Internally, Docker Datacenter places some VMs on a Private network (nodes), and some, load balanced by an Elastic Load Balancer (ELBs, for controllers), on which it installs the commercially supported version of the Engine. The current version of Docker Datacenter VMs run internally Swarm standalone and a discovery mechanism, to connect to each other. We can expect the stable version of Datacenter to be released soon.

The main difference between Docker Datacenter and Docker for AWS is that the first one is intended to be all-inclusive enterprise ready. While the latter is the fastest way to deploy specifically Swarm clusters, the first is more of a complete solution, with a fancy UI, Notary, and optional services from the ecosystem.

Swarm on OpenStack

Speaking of private cloud, the most popular open source solution for IaaS is OpenStack. OpenStack is a great ecosystem of programs (formerly known as projects), with the goal of providing a so-called cloud operating system. The core OpenStack programs are:

- **Keystone**: The identity and authorization system
- **Nova**: The virtual machine abstraction layer. Nova can be plugged with virtualization modules, such as Libvirt, VMware
- **Neutron**: The network module, which handles tenant networks, instances ports, routing, and traffic
- **Cinder**: The storage module responsible for handling volumes
- **Glance**: The image storage

Everything is glued up by additional actors:

- A database system, such as MySQL, keeping the configurations
- An AMQP broker, such as Rabbit, to queue and deliver operations
- A proxy system, such as HAproxy, to proxy HTTP API requests

In a typical VM creation in OpenStack, the following happens:

1. A user either from the UI (Horizon) or from the CLI decides to spawn a VM.
2. She/he clicks a button or types a command such as `nova boot` ...
3. Keystone checks authorization and authentication for this user in his/her tenant, by checking in the user's database or in LDAP (depends on how OpenStack is configured) and generates a token that will be used throughout the whole session: `Here is your token: gAAAAABX781dEiY2`.
4. If authentication succeeds and the user is authorized to spawn a VM, Nova is invoked by using the authorization token: "We are launching a VM, can you please find a suitable physical host where to?"
5. If such an host exists, Nova takes the image of choice of the user from Glance: "Glance, please pass me an Ubuntu Xenial bootable qcow2 file"
6. On the compute host where to physically launch the VM, a `nova-compute` process, which talks to the configured plugin, for example, says to Libvirt: "We are starting a VM on this host"
7. Neutron allocates private (and public, if required) network ports for the VM: "Please create these ports on the designated networks, in these subnet pools"
8. If the user wants to, Cinder allocates volume/s on the hosts designed by its scheduler. That is. Let's create additional volume/s and let's attach them to the VM.
9. If KVM is used, a suitable XML is generated with all the information above, and Libvirt starts the VM on the compute host
10. When the VM is started, some variables are injected via cloud-init, for example, an SSH key to allow passwordless SSH logins

This is (except for step 8 on Cinder) exactly how the OpenStack driver of Docker Machine behaves: when you create a Docker Host with Machine using `-d openstack`, you have to specify an existing glance image, an existing private (and optionally a public) network, and (optionally, otherwise is automatically generated) specify an SSH image, stored in the Nova database. And, of course, you have to pass to Machine the authorization variables to your OpenStack environment, or alternatively, source them as exported shell variables.

A Machine command creating a Docker Host on OpenStack will then look like this:

```
docker-machine create \
--driver openstack \
--openstack-image-id 98011e9a-fc46-45b6-ab2c-cf6c43263a22 \
--openstack-flavor-id 3 \
--openstack-floatingip-pool public \
--openstack-net-id 44ead515-da4b-443b-85cc-a5d13e06ddc85 \
--openstack-sec-groups machine \
--openstack-ssh-user ubuntu \
ubuntu1
```

OpenStack Nova

So, the classical way to go for Docker Swarm on OpenStack would be starting creating instances, say 10 VMs from Ubuntu 16.04 images, on a dedicated network:

- From the web UI, specifying 10 as the number of instances
- Or from the CLI, using `nova boot ... --max-count 10 machine-`
- Or by using Docker Machine

The last is the more promising way because Machine automatically installs Docker, without later having to hack or have to use other tools on the newly created instances (such as Machine with the generic driver, Belt, Ansible, Salt or other scripts). But at the time of writing (Machine 0.8.2), Machine does not support bulk-host creations, so you will have to loop a `docker-machine` command with some basic shell logic:

```
#!/bin/bash
for i in `seq 0 9`; do
        docker-machine create -d openstack ... openstack-machine-$i
done
```

This is not a good UX at all, also because Machine scales still very bad when we speak of dozens of hosts.

The (deprecated) nova-docker driver

Once, there was a driver for Nova, to plug Docker containers as final destinations for Nova (instead of creating KVM or VmWare VMs, for example, these drivers allowed to create and manage Docker containers from Nova). If using such a tool for the *old* Swarm makes sense (since everything is orchestrated as containers), this is of no interest for Swarm Mode, which needs Docker Hosts rather than bare containers.

The reality – OpenStack the friendly way

Luckily, OpenStack is a very vibrant project, and now that it has reached release **O** (**Ocata**), it is enriched by many optional modules. From the Docker Swarm perspective, the most interesting ones are:

- **Heat:** This is the orchestrator system, which can create VMs configurations from templates.
- **Murano:** This is the application catalog that can run applications from a catalog maintained by the open source community, including Docker and Kubernetes containers.
- **Magnum:** This is the Container as a Service solution from Rackspace.
- **Kuryr:** This is the networking abstractor. With Kuryr, you can link Neutron tenant networks and Docker networks created with Docker Libnetwork (such as the Swarm ones), and connect OpenStack instances with Docker containers as if they were connected to the same network.

OpenStack Heat

OpenStack Heat resembles Docker Compose a bit, allowing you to start systems by a template, but it's much more powerful: You can not only boot a set of instances from an image, say Ubuntu 16.04, but you can orchestrate them, which means create networks, attach VMs interfaces to networks, place load balancers and execute later tasks on the instances, such as installing Docker. Roughly, Heat is the equivalent of Amazon's CloudFormation for OpenStack.

In Heat everything starts from YAML templates, thanks to which you can model your infrastructure, before firing it up, in the same fashion as you do with Compose. For example, you create a template file like this:

```
. . .
resources:
  dockerhosts_group:
    type: OS::Heat::ResourceGroup
    properties:
      count: 10
      resource_def:
        type: OS::Nova::Server
        properties:
          # create a unique name for each server
          # using its index in the group
          name: docker_host_%index%
```

```
image: Ubuntu 16.04
flavor: m.large
```
. . .

Then, you can launch a stack from it (`heat stack-create -f configuration.hot dockerhosts`). Heat will call Nova, Neutron, Cinder and all the necessary OpenStack services to orchestrate resources and make them available.

Here we're not going to show how to start a Docker Swarm infrastructure through Heat, rather we'll see here Magnum, which uses Heat underneath to manipulate OpenStack objects.

OpenStack Magnum

Magnum, announced in late 2015 and developed by the OpenStack Containers Team, aims to make **Container Orchestration Engines** (**COEs**) such as Docker Swarm and **Kubernetes** available as first class resources in OpenStack. There were and there will be many projects inside the OpenStack arena focused to provide containers support, but Magnum goes further, because it's designed to support *containers orchestration*, not bare containers management.

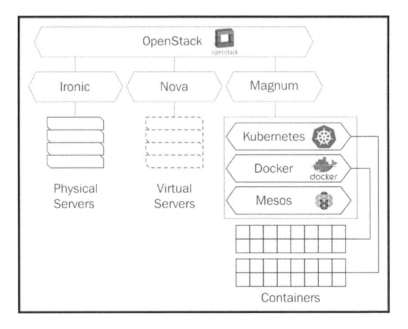

So far, the focus has been put especially on Kubernetes, but we're speaking of **Magnum** here because it's the most promising open source technology for providing a convenient way of running CaaS orchestration on the private cloud. Magnum does not support the newest Swarm Mode yet, at the time of writing: This feature must be addressed. There is a Launchpad blueprint opened by the author, who eventually might start working on after the book is published:

`https://blueprints.launchpad.net/magnum/+spec/swarm-mode-support`.

Architecture and core concepts

Magnum has two main components, running on controller nodes:

```
magnum-api
magnum-conductor
```

The first process, `magnum-api` is the typical OpenStack API provider, invoked by the magnum Python client or by other processes for operations, such as creating a cluster. The latter, `magnum-conductor`, is invoked by `magnum-api` (more or less, it has the same functions of `nova-conductor`) through an AMQP server, such as Rabbit, and its goal is to interface to the Kubernetes or Docker APIs. In practice, these two binaries work together to provide a sort of orchestration abstraction.

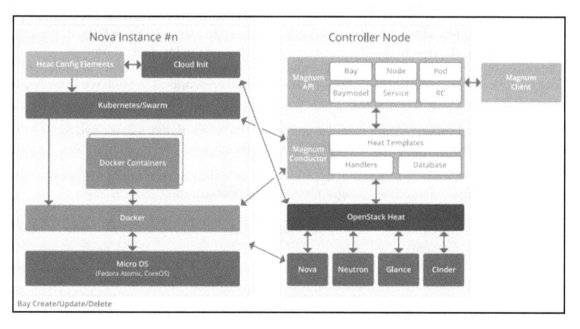

On the OpenStack cluster compute nodes, nothing special is necessary to run, apart from `nova-compute` processes: Magnum conductor exploits Heat directly to create stacks, which creates networks and instantiates VMs in Nova.

The Magnum terminology is evolving alongside with the project. But these are the main concepts:

- **Containers** are Docker containers.
- A **Cluster** (formerly a Bay) is a collection of node objects where work is scheduled, for example, Swarm nodes.
- A **ClusterTemplate** (formerly BayModel) is the template storing information about the cluster types. For example, a ClusterTemplate defines *a Swarm cluster with 3 managers and 5 workers*.
- **Pods** are a collection of containers running on the same physical or virtual machine.

As for advanced options, such as storage, new COEs support, and scaling, Magnum is a very active project and we recommend you to follow its evolution on `http://docs.openstack.org/developer/magnum/`.

Install HA Magnum on Mirantis OpenStack

Installing Magnum is not so trivial, especially if you want to warranty some failover typical of OpenStack HA deployments. There are many tutorials on the Internet on how to configure Magnum in DevStack (the developer's 1-node staging setup), but none showing how to work on real production systems with more than one controller. Here we show how to install Magnum on a real setup..

Typically, production OpenStack installations count a number of nodes dedicated to different goals. In a minimal HA deployment, there usually are:

- Three or more (odd number for quorum reasons) **controller nodes**, responsible of hosting the OpenStack program's APIs and configuration services, such as Rabbit, MySQL, and HAproxy
- An arbitrary number of **compute nodes**, where workloads run physically (where VMs are hosted)

Optionally, there may be dedicated storage, monitoring, database, network, and other nodes.

In our setup here, based on **Mirantis OpenStack** running Newton with Heat installed, we have three controllers and three computes plus storage nodes. HA is configured with Pacemaker, which keeps resources as MySQL, Rabbitmq, and HAproxy in high availability. APIs are proxied by HAproxy. This is a screenshot showing the resources configured into Pacemaker. They all are started and working properly:

```
                              1. root@node-2: ~ (ssh)
root@node-2:~# pcs resource
 Clone Set: clone_p_vrouter [p_vrouter]
     Started: [ node-2.domain.local node-3.domain.local node-7.domain.local ]
 vip__management          (ocf::fuel:ns_IPaddr2): Started node-2.domain.local
 vip__vrouter_pub         (ocf::fuel:ns_IPaddr2): Started node-2.domain.local
 vip__vrouter   (ocf::fuel:ns_IPaddr2): Started node-2.domain.local
 vip__public    (ocf::fuel:ns_IPaddr2): Started node-3.domain.local
 Clone Set: clone_p_haproxy [p_haproxy]
     Started: [ node-2.domain.local node-3.domain.local node-7.domain.local ]
 Clone Set: clone_p_mysqld [p_mysqld]
     Started: [ node-2.domain.local node-3.domain.local node-7.domain.local ]
 Master/Slave Set: master_p_conntrackd [p_conntrackd]
     Masters: [ node-2.domain.local ]
     Slaves: [ node-3.domain.local node-7.domain.local ]
 sysinfo_node-2.domain.local    (ocf::pacemaker:SysInfo):     Started node-2.domain.local
 sysinfo_node-3.domain.local    (ocf::pacemaker:SysInfo):     Started node-3.domain.local
 Master/Slave Set: master_p_rabbitmq-server [p_rabbitmq-server]
     Masters: [ node-3.domain.local ]
     Slaves: [ node-2.domain.local node-7.domain.local ]
 Clone Set: clone_neutron-openvswitch-agent [neutron-openvswitch-agent]
     Started: [ node-2.domain.local node-3.domain.local node-7.domain.local ]
 Clone Set: clone_neutron-l3-agent [neutron-l3-agent]
     Started: [ node-2.domain.local node-3.domain.local node-7.domain.local ]
 Clone Set: clone_neutron-metadata-agent [neutron-metadata-agent]
     Started: [ node-2.domain.local node-3.domain.local node-7.domain.local ]
 Clone Set: clone_neutron-dhcp-agent [neutron-dhcp-agent]
     Started: [ node-2.domain.local node-3.domain.local node-7.domain.local ]
 Clone Set: clone_p_dns [p_dns]
     Started: [ node-2.domain.local node-3.domain.local node-7.domain.local ]
 sysinfo_node-1.domain.local    (ocf::pacemaker:SysInfo):     Stopped
 Clone Set: clone_ping_vip__public [ping_vip__public]
     Started: [ node-2.domain.local node-3.domain.local node-7.domain.local ]
 Clone Set: clone_p_ntp [p_ntp]
     Started: [ node-2.domain.local node-3.domain.local node-7.domain.local ]
 sysinfo_node-7.domain.local    (ocf::pacemaker:SysInfo):     Started node-7.domain.local
root@node-2:~#
```

All nodes in the cluster run Ubuntu 16.04 (Xenial), for which the stable Magnum 2.0 packages exist, so it's enough to consume them from upstream and install with `apt-get install`.

Before installing Magnum, however, it's necessary to prepare the environment. First, a database is required. Enter the MySQL console from any controller by just typing:

```
node-1# mysql
```

In MySQL, create the magnum database and user, and grant the correct privileges:

```
CREATE DATABASE magnum;
GRANT ALL PRIVILEGES ON magnum.* TO 'magnum'@'controller' \
   IDENTIFIED BY 'password';
GRANT ALL PRIVILEGES ON magnum.* TO 'magnum'@'%' \
   IDENTIFIED BY 'password';
```

Now, it's necessary to create the service credentials in Keystone, beginning with defining a magnum OpenStack user, who must be added to the services group. The services group is a special group, which includes the OpenStack services running across the cluster, such as Nova, Neutron, and so on.

```
openstack user create --domain default --password-prompt magnum
openstack role add --project services --user magnum admin
```

After that, a new service must be created:

```
openstack service create --name magnum \    --description "OpenStack
Container Infrastructure" \    container-infra
```

OpenStack programs are invoked and talk through their APIs. An API is accessed with an endpoint, that is a pair URL and port, which in HA setups is proxied by HAproxy. In our setup, HAproxy receives HTTP requests on `10.21.22.2.` and balances them across the controller IPs, that are `10.21.22.4,` 5, and 6.

```
1. root@node-2: ~ (ssh)
root@node-2:~# cat /etc/haproxy/conf.d/040-nova-api.cfg | egrep "listen|bind|node"
listen nova-api
  bind 10.21.22.2:8774
    server node-2 10.21.22.5:8774  check inter 10s fastinter 2s downinter 3s rise 3 fall 3
    server node-3 10.21.22.4:8774  check inter 10s fastinter 2s downinter 3s rise 3 fall 3
    server node-7 10.21.22.6:8774  check inter 10s fastinter 2s downinter 3s rise 3 fall 3
root@node-2:~#
```

We have to create such endpoints for Magnum, which listens by default on port 9511, for each zone (public, internal, and admin):

```
openstack endpoint create --region RegionOne \
  container-infra public http://10.21.22.2:9511/v1
openstack endpoint create --region RegionOne \
  container-infra internal http://10.21.22.2:9511/v1
openstack endpoint create --region RegionOne \
  container-infra admin http://10.21.22.2:9511/v1
```

Also, Magnum needs an additional configuration to organize its workloads internally in domains, so a dedicated domain plus a domain user must be added:

```
openstack domain create --description "Magnum" magnum
openstack user create --domain magnum --password-prompt
magnum_domain_admin
openstack role add --domain magnum --user magnum_domain_admin admin
```

Now everything is in place to finally run `apt-get`. On all three controllers, run the following command and in the ncurses interface, always answer No, to not change the environment, or keep the default configurations:

```
apt-get install magnum-api magnum-conductor
```

Configure an HA Magnum installation

The configuration of Magnum is pretty straightforward. What's needed to be done to have it in an up and running state is:

1. Configure it through the `magnum.conf` file.
2. Restart the magnum binaries.
3. Open port `tcp/9511`.
4. Configure HAproxy to accept and balance magnum APIs.
5. Reload HAproxy.

The crucial configurations that must be done on each controller follow. First, on every controller the host parameter should be the IP of the interface on the management network:

```
[api]
host = 10.21.22.6
```

If **Barbican** (the OpenStack project dedicated to the management of secrets such as password) is not installed, certificates must be handled by the **x509keypair** plugin:

```
[certificates]
cert_manager_type = x509keypair
```

Then, a database connection string is required. In this HA setup, MySQL answers on the VIP 10.21.22.2:

```
[database]
connection=mysql://magnum:password@10.21.22.2/magnum
```

The Keystone authentication is configured as follow (the options are rather self-explanatory):

```
[keystone_authtoken]
auth_uri=http://10.21.22.2:5000/
memcached_servers=10.21.22.4:11211,
10.21.22.5:11211,10.21.22.6:11211
auth_type=password
username=magnum
project_name=services
auth_url=http://10.21.22.2:35357/
password=password
user_domain_id = default
project_domain_id = default
auth_host = 127.0.0.1
auth_protocol = http
admin_user = admin
admin_password =
admin_tenant_name = admin
```

Oslo (the message broker) must be configured to messaging:

```
[oslo_messaging_notifications]
driver = messaging
```

The Rabbitmq configuration is this, specifying the Rabbit cluster hosts (since Rabbit runs on controllers, the IPs of all controllers' management network):

```
[oslo_messaging_rabbit]
rabbit_hosts=10.21.22.6:5673, 10.21.22.4:5673, 10.21.22.5:5673
rabbit_ha_queues=True
heartbeat_timeout_threshold=60
heartbeat_rate=2
rabbit_userid=magnum
rabbit_password=A3elbTUIqOcqRihB6XE3MWzN
```

Finally, an additional configuration of the trustee is as follows:

```
[trust]
trustee_domain_name = magnum
trustee_domain_admin_name = magnum_domain_admin
trustee_domain_admin_password = magnum
```

After this reconfiguration, the Magnum services must be restarted:

```
service magnum-api restart
service magnum-conductor restart
```

Magnum uses by default port `tcp/9511`, so traffic to this port must be accepted in iptables:
Modify iptables to add this rule:

```
-A INPUT -s 10.21.22.0/24 -p tcp -m multiport --dports 9511 -m
comment --comment "117 magnum-api from 10.21.22.0/24" -j ACCEPT
```

Just after the other OpenStack services, right after `116 openvswitch db`.

Now, it's time to configure HAproxy to accept magnum. Add an `180-magnum.cfg` file into
`/etc/haproxy/conf.d` on all controllers with this content:

```
listen magnum-api
  bind 10.21.22.2:9511
  http-request  set-header X-Forwarded-Proto https if { ssl_fc }
  option  httpchk
  option  httplog
  option  httpclose
  option  http-buffer-request
  timeout  server 600s
  timeout  http-request 10s
  server node-1 10.21.22.6:9511  check inter 10s fastinter 2s
  downinter 3s rise 3 fall 3
  server node-2 10.21.22.5:9511  check inter 10s fastinter 2s
  downinter 3s rise 3 fall 3
  server node-3 10.21.22.4:9511  check inter 10s fastinter 2s
  downinter 3s rise 3 fall 3
```

This configures the magnum-api to listen on the VIP `10.21.22.2:9511`, backing on the
three controllers.

Just right after, HAproxy must be restarted from Pacemaker. From any controller, run:

```
pcs resource disable p_haproxy
```

Wait until no HAproxy processes are running on all controllers (you can check with `ps aux`), but this should be very fast, less than 1 second, then:

```
pcs resource enable p_haproxy
```

After that, Magnum will be available with services up:

```
source openrc
magnum service-list
```

```
root@node-2:~# magnum service-list
+----+------------------------------+------------------+-------+----------+-----------------+---------------------------+---------------------------+
| id | host                         | binary           | state | disabled | disabled_reason | created_at                | updated_at                |
+----+------------------------------+------------------+-------+----------+-----------------+---------------------------+---------------------------+
| 2  | messaging-node-3.domain.local | magnum-conductor | up    |          | -               | 2016-10-02T13:11:54+00:00 | 2016-10-02T14:27:10+00:00 |
| 4  | node-2.domain.local          | magnum-conductor | up    |          | -               | 2016-10-02T13:11:58+00:00 | 2016-10-02T14:27:22+00:00 |
| 6  | node-7.domain.local          | magnum-conductor | up    |          | -               | 2016-10-02T14:22:15+00:00 | 2016-10-02T14:27:32+00:00 |
+----+------------------------------+------------------+-------+----------+-----------------+---------------------------+---------------------------+
root@node-2:~#
```

Create a Swarm cluster on Magnum

Creating a Swarm cluster, when the COE will be added to Magnum, will require these steps:

1. Create a Swarm Mode template.
2. Launch a cluster from the template.

We're not diving too much into something that doesn't exist yet, but the commands will be something like this:

```
magnum cluster-template-create \
--name swarm-mode-cluster-template \
--image-id ubuntu_xenial \
--keypair-id fuel \
--fixed-network private \
--external-network-id public \
--dns-nameserver 8.8.8.8 \
--flavor-id m1.medium \
--docker-volume-size 5 \
--coe swarm-mode
```

Here, a cluster template of type swarm-mode based on Ubuntu Xenial with `m1.medium` flavors is defined: VMs will be injected the fuel keypair, will have an additional external public IP. The UX for creating a cluster based on such a template might be expected to be:

```
magnum cluster-create --name swarm-mode-cluster \
      --cluster-template swarm-mode-cluster-template \
      --manager-count 3 \
      --node-count 8
```

Here, a Swarm cluster is instantiated with three managers and five workers.

Magnum is a great project, at the highest level of abstraction for running container orchestration on OpenStack. It's running on the Rackspace cloud, and it's available for public usage through Carina, refer to `http://blog.rackspace.com/carina-by-rackspace-simplifies-containers-with-easy-to-use-instant-on-native-container-environment`.

Summary

In this chapter, we explored the alternative platforms on which we can run Docker Swarm clusters. We worked with the newest Docker tools–Docker for AWS and Docker for Azure–and we used them to demonstrate how to install Swarm in a new fashion. After introducing Docker Datacenter, we moved to the private cloud part. We worked on OpenStack, showing how to run Docker hosts on it, how to install OpenStack Magnum, and how to create Swarm objects on it. We've almost finished our travel.

The next and last chapter will sketch the future of Docker orchestration.

11
What is next?

The Docker ecosystem is converging towards a bigger picture, of which Swarm will be one of the core components. Let's hypothesize a roadmap.

The challenge of provisioning

There are no official tools to create a big Swarm at a scale yet. At the moment, operators use internal scripts, ad hoc tools (such as Belt), configuration managers (such as Puppet or Ansible), or orchestration templates (such as CloudFormation for AWS or Heat for OpenStack), as we have seen in the previous chapters. Recently, Docker For AWS and Azure came as alternatives.

But this use case will be probably addressed in a unified way with software-defined infrastructure toolkits.

Software defined infrastructure

Starting from containers as building blocks to then creating systems to architect, orchestrate, scale, secure, and deploy not only apps but also infrastructures, as a long-term goal there is probably the *programmable Internet*.

After SwarmKit, that's the kit for orchestration, Docker open sourced in October 2016 **Infrakit**, the kit for infrastructures.

Infrakit

While the focus of Docker Engine is containers and the focus of Docker Swarm is orchestration, the focus of Infrakit is on *groups* as primitives. Groups are intended of any object: Pets, cattle, unikernels, and Swarm clusters.

Infrakit is the answer to the problem of managing Docker in different infrastructures. Before Infrakit, this was difficult and not portable. The idea is to provide a consistent user experience from architecting data centers to run bare containers. Infrakit is the current highest level abstraction for creating programmable infrastructures by Docker and it describes itself as:

> *"InfraKit is a toolkit for creating and managing declarative, self-healing infrastructure. It breaks infrastructure automation down into simple, pluggable components. These components work together to actively ensure the infrastructure state matches the user's specifications."*

Infrakit in the stack leans against the flank of container engines.

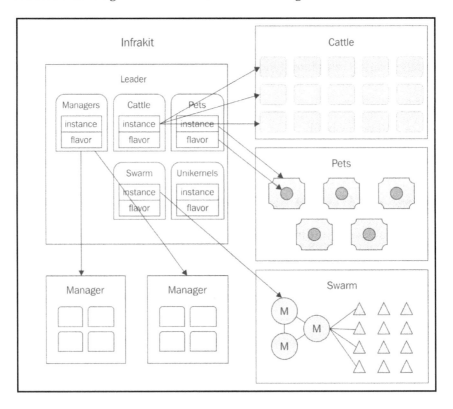

The organization is per groups. There is a group for the Infrakit itself structure, made of managers keeping a configuration. There is exactly one leader at a time, and some followers, for instance, have two. Every manager includes some group declarations. Groups may be of cattle, pets, swarms, unikernels, and so on. Every group is defined with instances (the real resources, for example, containers), and flavors (the type of resource, for example, Ubuntu Xenial or a MySQL Docker image).

Infrakit is declarative. It relies on a JSON configuration and internally uses the well-known patterns of encapsulation and composition to make configurations as inputs to process and make infrastructures to converge to a specific configuration.

The goals of Infrakit are to:

- Provide a unified toolkit to manage groups
- Be pluggable
- Provide self healing
- Release rolling updates

Groups abstract the notion of objects. They can be groups of any size and scale up, and down, they can be groups of named pets, unnamed cattle, Infrakit managers itself and/or all the above together. At the moment, in Infrakit there is only one default group configuration (the default plugin), but new group definitions may come later. The default group is an interface exposing actions such as watch/unwatch (start and stop groups), perform/stop updates, change group size.

Groups are made of instances. They may be physical resources such as VMs or containers, or interfaces to other services, such as Terraform.

On instances you can run flavors, for example, Zookeeper, MySQL, or Ubuntu Xenial.

Groups, instances, and flavors are pluggable: They run in fact as plugins that can be written in any language. At the moment, Infrakit ships some Go code, that when compiled gives a set of binaries, such as cli, which can be used to control, inspect, and perform operations on groups, instances, and flavors, and plugin binaries, such as terraform, swarm, or zookeeper.

Infrakit is thought to be able to manage inconsistencies, by continuously monitoring, detecting anomalies, and triggering actions. This propriety is called self-healing and can be used to create more robust systems.

One of the major operations supported by Infrakit will be releasing rolling updates to update instances. For example, update a package in a container, update a container image, or others maybe by using **TUF** (**The Update Framework**), a project described in the next section.

Infrakit is so early and young at the time of writing that we can't show any example that's not a Hello World. On the Internet, it will be soon full of Infrakit Hello Worlds, and the Infrakit team itself released a step-by-step tutorial to use it with the file or Terraform plugins. We can just depict it as the architectural layer in the Docker ecosystem and expect it to be able to deploy even Swarms, provisioning the hosts and interconnecting them.

Infrakit is expected to be included into the Engine, maybe as experimental in version 1.14.

TUF – The Update Framework

At Docker Summit 16 in Berlin, another topic was discussed, TUF (`https://theupdateframework.github.io/`), a toolkit which has the goal to provide a secure way to roll updates.

There are many update tools available, which do the update in practice, but TUF is much more. From the project's home page:

> *"TUF helps developers to secure new or existing software update systems, which are often found to be vulnerable to many known attacks. TUF addresses this widespread problem by providing a comprehensive, flexible security framework that developers can integrate with any software update system."*

TUF is already integrated into Docker, and the tool is called Notary, as we saw in `Chapter 9`, *Securing a Swarm Cluster and the Docker Software Supply Chain*, Notary can be used. Notary can be used to verify content and make the keys management easy. With Notary, developers can sign their content offline using keys and later make the content available, by pushing their signed trusted collection to a Notary Server.

Will TUF be merged into Docker Infrakit as the rolling update mechanism? That would be another amazing step ahead.

Docker stacks and Compose

Another Docker feature available to developers but still in experimental phase is Stacks. We introduced Stacks in `Chapter 6`, *Deploy Real Applications on Swarm*. They will become the default method of deploying applications on swarms. Instead of putting in motion containers, the idea is that groups of containers, packed into bundles, will be rather launched.

Also, a new integration between Compose and the new Swarm may be expected.

CaaS – Containers as a Service

In the XaaS arena, where everything is treated as a software, not only are containers first class citizens, but orchestration systems and infrastructures will also be. All these abstractions will lead to a cloud-defined way of running this ecosystem of tools: Containers as a Service.

An example of CaaS is the Docker Datacenter.

Unikernels

SwarmKit, as a kit, will run clusters not only of containers, but also unikernels, we said.

What are unikernels and why are they so fantastic?

If you use Docker For Mac, you're already using unikernels. They are the core of these systems. On Mac, **xhyve,** a port of the FreeBSD virtualization system **(bhyve),** runs a Docker host in unikernel mode.

We all love containers, because they are small and fast, but the security implications of having a mechanism abstracting the kernel and make its components (containers) to share system resources, libraries, binaries, are really a concern. Just look for CVEs bulletins regarding containers security on any search engine. That's a serious issue.

Unikernels promise a reassessment of software architecture at the highest level. This is quickly explained here. There is an efficient way to guarantee maximum security and because of their nature they run at a very very tiny size. In a world where we speak of Terabytes, Petabytes, and beyond, it will surprise you to know that a unikernel implementation of KVM like ukvm can fit in 67Kb (Kilobytes), web server binaries in 300Kb, or operating system images in order of some Megabytes.

This is possible because unikernels basically don't expose all the system calls to the stack, but those calls are included into the binary itself. A **ping** binary does not require any system call to access the disk, use cryptographic functions or manage system processes. So just why not cut off these calls to ping, and provide it with the minimal it requires? That's the main idea behind unikernels. A ping command will be compiled with *inside* some network I/O, raw sockets, and that's all.

With unikernels, there is no distinction between kernel and user space, as the address table is unified. This means that the address table is *continuous*. As explained earlier, this is possible because unikernel binaries are compiled embedding the system functions they need, such as I/O operations, memory management or shared libraries, *inside* the binary. In the traditional operating systems model, applications look and use the system calls at *runtime*, while with unikernels, these system calls are statically linked at *compile time*.

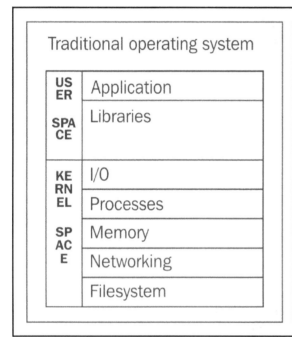
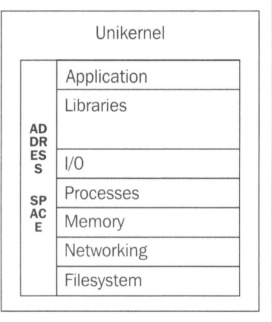

This can look strange at first sight but it's a tremendous advance in terms of process isolation and security. Even if someone is able to fraudulently introduce into some system running unikernel stuff, it's almost impossible for her to find any security breach. The attack surface is so minimal that it's highly improbable that there will be any exploitable unused system call or features, apart from the ones in use, possibly already hardened. There is no shell to invoke, there are no external utility libraries or scripts, there are no configuration or password files, there are no extra ports bind.

So what about unikernels and Docker?

At the DockerConEU 15 in Barcelona, some folks jump to the stage to show how to integrate Docker with unikernels, and later eventually Docker Inc. acquired the company, signing between the other things the birth of Docker For Mac.

At the Docker Summit 16 in Berlin, someone mentioned about unikernels running alongside with containers in SwarmKit. A future of integration is coming.

Contribute to Docker

All this innovation in Docker is possible because the projects rely on a very broad community. Docker is a very intense and active project, split into several Github repositories, the most notable of which are:

- Docker itself, the engine: `www.github.com/docker/docker`
- Machine, the Docker hosts instantiator: `www.github.com/docker/machine`
- Swarm, the orchestration service: `www.github.com/docker/swarmkit`
- Compose, the tool to model micro services: `www.github.com/docker/compose`
- Infrakit, the infrastructure manager: `www.github.com/docker/infrakit`

But also, these projects would not run without their libraries, such as Libcontainer, Libnetwork, Libcompose (waiting to be merged with Compose), and many many others.

All this code would not exist without the commitment of the Docker team and the Docker community.

Github

Any company or individual is encouraged to contribute to the projects. There are some guidelines at `https://github.com/docker/docker/blob/master/CONTRIBUTING.md`.

File issues

One great way to start is to report anomalies, bugs, or submit ideas, by opening issues on the GitHub space of the related project.

Code

Another well-appreciated way to help is to submit pull requests to either fix things or propose new features. These PRs should follow and reference to some issue recorded into the Issues page, accordingly to the guidelines.

Belt and other projects

Also, along with this books many mini side projects started:

- Swarm2k and Swarm3k, as community-oriented experiments to create Swarms at a scale. Some code, instructions, and results are available in the `www.github.com/swarmzilla` respective repositories.
- Belt as a Docker host provisioner. At the moment, it includes only the DigitalOcean driver, but it can be further extended.
- Ansible modules for Swarm, Machine, and Docker certificates, to be used in Ansible play books.
- Containers pushed to the Docker Hub to illustrate specific components (such as `fsoppelsa/etcd`) or introduce new features (such as `fsoppelsa/swarmkit`).
- Other minor pull requests, hacks and code portions..

In the spirit of open source, all of the above are free software and any contribution, improvement, or critic is very well appreciated.

Summary

Finally, a couple of words on the history of this book and a note on how astonishingly fast is the development of Docker.

When the project of writing a book on Docker Swarm was just drafted, at the day there was only the old Docker Swarm standalone mode, where a Swarm container was responsible for orchestrating infrastructures of containers, having to rely on external discovery systems, such as Etcd, Consul, or Zookeeper.

Looking back at these times, just some months ago, is like thinking to prehistory. Just later in June, when SwarmKit was open sourced as an orchestration kit and it was included into the Engine as Swarm Mode, a major step ahead was made by the Docker in terms of orchestration. A full, scalable and secure by default, and easy way to orchestrate Docker natively was released. Then, it turned out that the best way of orchestrating Docker was just Docker itself.

But when Infrakit was open sourced in October 2016, a new big step ahead was done in terms of infrastructure: now not only orchestrations and group of containers are primitives, but also groups of other objects, even mixed in the original Infrakit intent, are: Containers, VMs, unikernels, and possibly bare metal.

In the (near) future, we can expect all of these projects to be glued, having Infrakit as the infrastructure manager, capable of provisioning Swarms (of anything), where containers or other objects are orchestrated, interconnected, stored (state fully), roll updated, interconnected by overlay networks, and secured.

Swarm is just the beginning of this big-picture ecosystem.

Index